The Intelligent, Responsive Leader

The Intelligent, Responsive Leader

Steven Katz

Lisa Ain Dack

John Malloy

A SAGE Publishing Company

ONTARIO
PRINCIPALS'
COUNCIL
Exemplary Leadership in Public Education

FOR INFORMATION:

Corwin
A SAGE Company
2455 Teller Road
Thousand Oaks, California 91320
(800) 233-9936
www.corwin.com

SAGE Publications Ltd.
1 Oliver's Yard
55 City Road
London EC1Y 1SP
United Kingdom

SAGE Publications India Pvt. Ltd.
B 1/I 1 Mohan Cooperative Industrial Area
Mathura Road, New Delhi 110 044
India

SAGE Publications Asia-Pacific Pte. Ltd.
3 Church Street
#10-04 Samsung Hub
Singapore 049483

Executive Editor: Arnis Burvikovs
Senior Associate Editor: Desirée A. Bartlett
Editorial Assistant: Kaitlyn Irwin
Production Editor: Amy Schroller
Copy Editor: Judy Selhorst
Typesetter: C&M Digitals (P) Ltd.
Proofreader: Bonnie Moore
Indexer: Amy Murphy
Cover Designer: Gail Buschman
Marketing Manager: Nicole Franks

Printed in the United States of America

Library of Congress Cataloging-in-Publication Data

Names: Katz, Steven (College teacher), author. | Dack, Lisa A., author. | Malloy, John Patrick, author.

Title: Leading intelligent, responsive schools / Steven Katz, Lisa Ain Dack, John Malloy.

Description: Thousand Oaks, California : Corwin, 2017. | Includes bibliographical references and index.

Identifiers: LCCN 2017001554 | ISBN 9781506333151 (pbk. : alk. paper)

Subjects: LCSH: Educational leadership. | School management and organization. | School improvement programs. | Professional learning communities. | Teachers—In-service training.

Classification: LCC LB2806 .K279 2017 | DDC 371.2—dc23
LC record available at https://lccn.loc.gov/2017001554

This book is printed on acid-free paper.

17 18 19 20 21 10 9 8 7 6 5 4 3 2 1

Contents

Preface   ix
   The Rationale   ix
   The Focus   ix
   Organization   x
   Reading and Using This Book   xi

Acknowledgments   xiii
   Publisher's Acknowledgments

About the Authors   xv

Chapter 1: The Challenge of Leading in
the Middle Space   1

   Beyond Intentional Interruption   1
   The Centrality of Professional Learning   3
   Leading in the Middle Space   5
   Implementation Challenges at the
      Nexus of Pressures and Supports   10
   Initiativitis and Literal Leadership   13
   Polemics in the Middle Space   16
   Time for Reflection   16

Chapter 2: The Intelligent, Responsive School   17

   The Power of *And*   18
   Prescription *and* Professional Judgment   20
   Intelligent Expectations   21
      Informed or Uninformed Prescription   23
   Responsive Conditions   24

The Relationship Between Intelligent
   and Responsive 28
Beyond Polemics 32
Time for Reflection 33

Chapter 3: Intelligent, Responsive
Leadership Practice 35

Leadership, Professional Learning, and
   Classroom Practice 38
Intelligent Leadership Practices 40
   Setting Direction 41
   Building Relationships and Developing People ... 44
   Developing the Organization 46
   Improving the Instructional Program 48
   Securing Accountability 52
Leading an Intelligent, Responsive School 55
Time for Reflection 57

Chapter 4: The Psychological Foundations of
"Getting Better" 59

The Psychological Foundations of
   Leadership Learning Inquiries 60
   The Power of Purposeful Practice 62
   Deep Understanding: The DNA of
      "Getting Better" 66
   The Essential Elements of Purposeful Practice ... 67
The Psychological Foundations of
   Collaborative Leader Learning 73
   The Default Practices of Collaboration 74
   From "Great Discussions" to Focused Learning
      Conversations: The Value of Protocols 80
Time for Reflection 83

Chapter 5: Getting Better at "Influence"
Through Leader Learning Inquiries 85

What Are Leader Learning Teams? 86
Leadership Learning Inquiries 87

Developing a Leadership Inquiry Question
    Using Our Leadership Inquiry Template   91
    The "What" of a Leadership Inquiry   94
    The "Who" of a Leadership Inquiry   100
The "How" of a Leadership Inquiry   103
    Embedding the Professional Learning
        Cycle in Our Leadership Inquiry Template   106
    Small, Narrow, and Frequent
        Leadership Learning Moves   115
Why Sticking With the Template Matters   118
Knowing When a Leadership Inquiry Is "Done"   124
Moving Forward   124
Time for Reflection   125

Chapter 6: Ensuring That Together Is Better   127

The Mechanics of the Leader Learning Team   127
The Ongoing Spirit of Critical Friendship   128
Our Learning Conversations Protocol:
    An Intentional Interruption Strategy for
    Enhanced Collaborative Learning   130
    Excerpt From Protocol Step 1   136
    Excerpt From Protocol Step 2   140
    Excerpt From Protocol Step 3   143
    Excerpt From Protocol Step 4   145
    Excerpt From Protocol Step 5   146
    Excerpt From Protocol Step 6   149
    Excerpt From Protocol Step 7   151
Toward a Preferred Future of the Intelligent,
    Responsive School   152
Time for Reflection   153

References   157

Index   163

Preface

THE RATIONALE

The evidence-based foundation of many (if not most) school improvement efforts is that student success follows from high-quality classroom practice. And high-quality classroom practice follows from *real* professional learning—the kind of professional learning that results in sustained or *permanent* changes to thinking, knowing, and doing. Impactful school leaders know how to create the conditions for teachers to learn what they need to learn, so that teachers in turn can create the conditions for students to learn what they need to learn. As we've watched school (and district) leaders work to improve schools, we've observed a pervasive leadership challenge of practice. Namely, in looking to add value by influencing professional learning efforts, school leaders find themselves caught between a set of top-down, district-level forces that prescribe professional learning and practice expectations and a set of bottom-up, practitioner-driven forces that favor experience-centered professional judgment. These dual forces seem to create an oppositional dynamic, with the school leader caught in the middle. What does it mean to lead within that space? Or, to put it more accurately, what does it mean to *learn* how to lead in that space?

THE FOCUS

This book takes up that question by advancing a concept of the school as a learning organization in which prescribed expectations and experiential professional judgment don't have to be (and in fact shouldn't be) oppositional and incompatible. We refer to this particular type of learning organization as an *intelligent, responsive school*. And this book unpacks what it means to *learn to lead* an intelligent, responsive school by developing intelligent, responsive leadership practice. The shift in phraseology for the desired objective, from "how to lead" to "*learn* how to lead," is especially significant. Despite the human propensity to take mental shortcuts to avoid thinking (Katz & Dack, 2013) and, therefore, to request a "how-to" algorithm, the learning *is* the work. The expertise research underscores the robust relationship between understanding and efficacy. Understanding predicts impact. Deeper understanding leads to better impact. Building a deep understanding of leadership as "influence" through an intentional and deliberate learning process that takes the form of "purposeful practice" is what it takes to develop intelligent, responsive leadership practice. There are no shortcuts, but the process outlined in this book charts the way forward.

ORGANIZATION

This book is organized into six chapters: In Chapter 1, "The Challenge of Leading in the Middle Space," we describe the challenge of being a principal occupying the middle space between the decentralized contextual realities of classroom teachers looking to learn through *bottom-up* professional judgment processes and the centralized efforts of *top-down* system prescription. In Chapter 2, "The Intelligent, Responsive School," we outline our concept of the intelligent, responsive school as a way of moving beyond the polemics that come from leading in the middle space. We recast the experiential tension as a creative one and assert that a certain kind of wisdom exists in the space between the perceived incompatibilities—namely, an opportunity for impactful professional learning. In Chapter 3, "Intelligent, Responsive Leadership Practice," we explain how intelligent, responsive schools require intelligent, responsive leadership, and we describe what such practice entails. In Chapter 4, "The Psychological Foundations of 'Getting Better,'" we unpack the conceptual underpinnings of our Leader Learning Team (LLT) structure and process for how leaders can go about building the requisite capacities to lead effectively through "influence." We explain the power of "purposeful practice" as a methodology for getting better, and we explore how deep understanding is at the core of what it means to get better. In Chapter 5, "Getting Better at 'Influence' Through Leader Learning Inquiries," we describe how adaptive challenges around the notion of "leadership as influence" are transformed into investigable leadership inquiry questions for the purposes of getting better. In Chapter 6, "Ensuring That Together Is Better," we highlight how groups of administrators engage in highly structured "critical friend" interactions to enable true professional learning in themselves and others.

READING AND USING THIS BOOK

This book is for educational leaders who are committed to answering two key questions in the service of developing their schools and/or districts as true learning organizations: Am *I* getting better? And how do *I* know? It unfolds according to a sequential story line, and as such it should be read straight through the first time. After that, it can be used and referenced in parts to guide learning and conversation among school and district teams. The education sphere is rife with occurrences in which tools travel more easily than their conceptual underpinnings. And when tools travel without their conceptual underpinnings, implementation suffers. There are lots of good ideas out there, but quality implementation is where the real work lies. Learning to influence others in the service of quality implementation defines a core leadership function. This book includes a practical set of tools designed to support this objective, but it keeps them attached to the "why" in order to enhance implementation efficacy. Wherever possible, we provide concrete, school-based illustrations of the ideas being described. These examples are all drawn from real practice and come from our own work and experience in researching and facilitating professional learning for leaders in many school districts over several decades. Each chapter finishes with a section headed "Time for Reflection," which presents a number of questions relating to major ideas in the chapter. These questions are designed to help readers reflect on and mobilize the content of each chapter in personal ways.

Acknowledgments

This book emerges from an iterative development and research process that focuses on learning about quality implementation in authentic contexts of actual practice. It wouldn't have been possible without the open-to-learning stance of our countless partners in the field who, like us, are committed to answering two key questions—Am I getting better? How do I know?—in visible and transparent ways. Our deep and consequential relationships with a host of school districts in the province of Ontario have been invaluable, and there are no shortcuts to the countless hours we've spent working and learning together to build capacity in support of student achievement. We are thankful for the privilege of being the ultimate insiders/outsiders in these jurisdictions, which has afforded us a unique and unparalleled vantage point from which to support—and learn about—growth and improvement. Directors of education, superintendents, administrators, consultants, coordinators, and teachers have often (bravely) invited us into their professional spaces and become our conversation partners and our friends. You know who you are, and this book could not have been possible without you.

PUBLISHER'S ACKNOWLEDGMENTS

Corwin gratefully acknowledges the contributions of the following reviewers:

Lynn Macan, Visiting Assistant Professor
University at Albany–SUNY
Albany, New York

Dr. Neil MacNeill, Headmaster
Ellenbrook Independent Primary School
Ellenbrook, Australia

Brigitte Tennis, Founder, Headmistress, and
    8th–10th Grade Teacher
Stella Schola Middle School
Redmond, Washington

About the
Authors

 Steven Katz is the director of Aporia Consulting Ltd. and a faculty member in Applied Psychology and Human Development at the Ontario Institute for Studies in Education of the University of Toronto (OISE, UT), where he teaches in the Child Study and Education graduate program. He is the recipient of the OISE, UT–wide award for teaching excellence. Steven has a PhD in human development and applied psychology, with a specialization in applied cognitive science. His areas of expertise include cognition and learning, teacher education, networked learning communities, leading professional learning, and evidence-informed decision making for school improvement. He has received the Governor General's Medal for excellence in his field and has been involved in research and evaluation, professional development, and consulting with a host of educational organizations around the world. He is an author of several best-selling books, including *Leading Schools in a Data-Rich World, Building and Connecting Learning Communities,* and *Intentional Interruption.*

Lisa Ain Dack is a senior associate at Aporia Consulting Ltd. and an instructor in the Master of Teaching and Master of Child Study and Education programs at the Ontario Institute for Studies in Education of the University of Toronto (OISE, UT). She has a PhD in developmental psychology and education from OISE, UT, with a collaborative degree in developmental science. She is the 2017 recipient of the OISE, UT award for excellence in Initial Teacher Education. Lisa facilitates Leader Learning Teams in various school districts in Ontario, leads numerous research projects investigating learning teams, and is involved in research projects on assessment and evaluation. She also undertakes program evaluations at both the primary and secondary levels. In addition, she leads workshops for administrators and teachers throughout Ontario on Leader Learning Teams, professional learning, and data-driven decision making. She is coauthor of the best-selling book *Intentional Interruption*. Lisa and her husband Jeff have three children, Sadie, Rachel, and Dylan.

John Malloy is the director of education for the Toronto District School Board. He has an EdD in educational administration from the University of Toronto (OISE, UT). Prior to his current position, he held senior leadership positions at the Ontario Ministry of Education and in three other Ontario school districts. His areas of expertise include leadership development, large-scale system change, strategic planning, professional learning, and equity. John has fostered a culture of collaborative inquiry and shared leadership in each of the school districts where he has served as a leader, which in turn has produced improved outcomes for students.

1

The Challenge of Leading in the Middle Space

In our previous book, *Intentional Interruption: Breaking Down Learning Barriers to Transform Professional Practice* (Katz & Dack, 2013), we articulate the links among professional learning, high-quality classroom practice, and improved student achievement. We explain that new professional learning—real learning—is hard work. We describe how human beings have a natural (but unconscious) propensity either to avoid new learning or to turn something novel into something familiar. That is, we transform the world to fit what's already in our minds. But what we are really after—real learning—involves changing our mental structures to fit new information that we encounter. New learning is about thinking, knowing, and understanding differently than we did before. In *Intentional Interruption*, we explain that if we are going to

1

facilitate *real* professional learning—what we call deep conceptual change—then it's important to understand what gets in the way. We suggest that successful school improvement is about intentional interruption—an intentional interruption of the subtle supports that work to preserve the status quo and impede new learning. And we outline what it means to intentionally interrupt the status quo of professional learning in order to enable *real* new learning that takes the form of permanent changes in thinking and practice.

Since the publication of *Intentional Interruption*, we have been part of many school districts' efforts to put the book's ideas into practice as a core part of their school improvement efforts and, in particular, their leadership development efforts. With much of the recent research on school leadership pointing to the impact and importance of instructional leadership (e.g., Hattie, 2015), the ability of leaders to lead real professional learning through intentional interruption has taken center stage. As we've said before, student success follows from high-quality classroom practice. High-quality classroom practice follows from real professional learning. Impactful school leaders know how to create the conditions for teachers to learn what they need to learn, so that teachers in turn can create the conditions for students to learn what they need to learn.

As we've joined many school (and district) leaders on their respective journeys to lead learning and improve schools, we've encountered a ubiquitous leadership problem of professional practice. Specifically, school leaders often find themselves situated between a set of top-down, district-level directives that prescribe expectations and a set of bottom-up, practitioner-driven preferences that favor experiential professional judgment. This duality seems to present often as an incompatibility, with the school leader caught in the middle. What does it mean to "lead" within that space? What does it mean to be a "learning organization" in that space? In this book we take up these questions by putting forth the notion of a school as a learning organization in which prescribed expectations and experiential professional judgment aren't oppositional and incompatible. We refer to this particular type of learning organization as an *intelligent, responsive school.*

Our goal in this book is to unpack what it means to effectively lead an intelligent, responsive school. Before we can do that, however, we need to do a couple of things fairly quickly: first, we need to revisit and reiterate the centrality of professional learning to the school improvement agenda, because it's at the heart of what impactful instructional leaders seek to influence; and second, we need to engage in the one practice that the literature on expertise suggests unites all experts regardless of domain—an in-depth understanding of the nature of the problem or challenge that we are up against. This chapter does both of those things.

THE CENTRALITY OF PROFESSIONAL LEARNING

We consider professional learning to be at the heart of all school improvement processes because it's at the heart of impactful practice. Professional learning that allows educators to grapple with complex challenges of practice, which grow out of student learning needs, has the best possibility of leading to different and effective ways of thinking and doing in schools. As we explain in *Intentional Interruption,* teacher practice is the single biggest predictor of student outcomes. If teacher practice doesn't change in classrooms where students are struggling to achieve, it's unlikely that student learning will improve. Real professional learning needs to drive this change. Real professional learning is much more than teachers planning lessons together, engaging in a book study, or even talking about the different challenges they face each day in their classrooms. The kind of professional learning that we are talking about here is that which is directed by a clear, needs-based focus and follows a professional learning cycle in a disciplined way. Figure 1.1 illustrates and explicates this process.

Figure 1.1   The Professional Learning Cycle

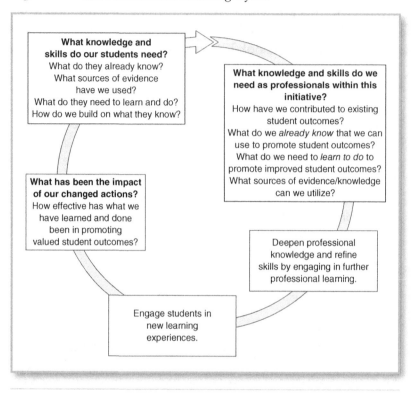

What knowledge and skills do our students need?
What do they already know?
What sources of evidence have we used?
What do they need to learn and do?
How do we build on what they know?

What knowledge and skills do we need as professionals within this initiative?
How have we contributed to existing student outcomes?
What do we *already know* that we can use to promote student outcomes?
What do we need to *learn to do* to promote improved student outcomes?
What sources of evidence/knowledge can we utilize?

What has been the impact of our changed actions?
How effective has what we have learned and done been in promoting valued student outcomes?

Deepen professional knowledge and refine skills by engaging in further professional learning.

Engage students in new learning experiences.

Source: Timperley, Wilson, Barrar, and Fung (2008).

Most teachers that we know work hard each and every day to provide the best opportunities for their students. They utilize all the strategies that they know to make a difference for the children in their care. Teachers don't purposefully hold back. If they know what to do to ensure that each student is achieving in their classrooms, they do it. They don't "save their best" for when students are more deserving! Research tells us that many teachers are good at knowing where students are struggling (Katz, Earl, & Ben Jaafar, 2009). The challenge is in knowing what to do for each student in the face of these learning gaps. We know that more of the same—even slower, louder, and a few more times—isn't likely to yield a different result. This is why professional learning matters so much. There are only two options for change: new students or new teaching practices. The former usually isn't possible. Parents aren't keeping the good students at home. They're sending the best they've got. So if teachers are teaching the best way they know how but there are still learning gaps for students, we need to think about changing teaching practice. That's where professional learning comes in.

The research-based theory of action that we explicate in *Intentional Interruption* (reproduced here in Figure 1.2) shows how positive impacts on student learning, achievement, and well-being are dependent on high-quality classroom practice, which, in turn, is dependent on impactful professional learning. The challenge, as we have explained, is that most professional learning doesn't result in changed thinking and practice in schools and classrooms because the new learning doesn't reach the requisite threshold for "permanence." *Permanence* refers to the extent to which the status quo of believing, thinking, and acting is changed forever. It doesn't prohibit continuing to grow and move forward, but it does preclude going "back" to previous patterns of knowing and doing. Richard Elmore's book title *I Used to Think . . . and Now I Think . . .* (2011) succinctly captures what we are getting at here. The details behind the what, how, and who of "real" or "permanent" professional learning are spelled out in *Intentional Interruption*, and we won't recapitulate them here. Suffice it to say, the necessary evidence-based professional learning focus and the requisite professional learning methodology that we refer to as "collaborative inquiry that challenges thinking and practice" are essential enablers of professional learning. School leaders— as instructional leaders—play a key role in creating the conditions for these things.

LEADING IN THE MIDDLE SPACE

Principals, as instructional leaders, play a significant role in creating the conditions for learning for both students and staff (see, e.g., Robinson, Hohepa, & Lloyd, 2009). As they work collaboratively with their colleagues to learn about creating

Figure 1.2   The Path of School Improvement

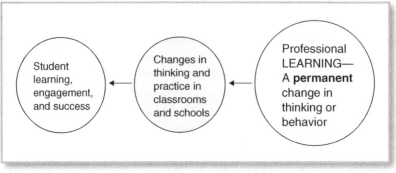

Source: Katz and Dack (2013).

effective conditions for teaching and learning, they also find themselves in the challenging position of supporting each and every teacher in their schools while responding to the many expectations that come from their communities, their school districts, and state or provincial bodies. Being a principal is challenging; on the worst days, it feels like there is little escape from the "pressures from above" and "blame from below." Leithwood and Azah (2014) have examined this phenomenon from a "workload" perspective, exploring the cognitive and emotional dimensions of workload pressures that principals feel while living in this space. But it is exactly in this "middle space" that principals do exercise their leadership, as they are the key link between the district's central office and the classroom. And as we know from the research, principal leadership is second only to teacher practice when it comes to influencing student learning and achievement (Leithwood, 2012). The middle space is challenging but important.

There are many examples to illustrate the challenges principals experience while leading in this middle space. Principals attend meetings where they learn about effective practice and hear expectations about school improvement efforts. They have opportunities to learn about what research says about good instruction and about the experiences of other colleagues in terms of their improvement efforts, and they are exposed to a myriad of initiatives (and resources) that have been created at the system level that are intended to assist them (even though they don't always experience the initiatives as such). These principals also have many responsibilities at their schools in terms of managing day-to-day operations, meeting with parents, mediating various conflicts involving students, and administering different procedures. Principals walk a very fine line because they are expected to be visible and public co-learners alongside their staffs (Robinson et al., 2009) while at the same time maintaining supervisory responsibilities over their staffs. Negotiating this power dynamic is not easy. Principals are dealing with individual teachers, their interests and needs; they are dealing with the collective staff and the culture of that staff; they are working closely with their district leaders, and maybe even a learning team of principals; and they are expected to fulfill the expectations that come not only from their districts but also from the state/ provincial level. Our observations across many school districts tell us that for principals, leading in this middle space often feels more frenetic and reactive than intentional. And without the "intentional," there is no "intentional interruption" of the status quo (in the service of the kind of professional learning that results in improved teaching practice).

AN IMAGE TO HOLD IN MIND

To illustrate the challenging dynamic we are describing, consider the experience of one principal in a school that we know well. It's an elementary school of approximately six hundred students and thirty teachers, in a socioeconomically challenged urban community. For many years the prevailing narrative within the school was that the social and emotional challenges that the students experience precluded the school's meeting their learning and achievement needs. Over the previous decade, whenever

(Continued)

(Continued)

principals or vice principals tried to bring about a change in student learning outcomes, their efforts were met with the kind of resistance that implied that these administrators did not truly understand the plight of the students that the school was serving. The teachers in the school were very committed to their students, and they worked tirelessly in the community and in the school on efforts that we would describe as serving a "culture of care." They defined their work—hard work—around important things like early-morning breakfast programs and winter coat drives, but it was difficult to see evidence of the kind of professional work focused on learning and teaching that might change learning outcomes for students. Furthermore, without intending to use a deficit lens when talking about their students, educators in this school did not seem to really *believe* that their students could attain higher levels of achievement. A culture of high expectations was absent. The teachers in the school were collegial with one another, but they did not believe that they had the collective capability to change life chances for their students. Most of the time, when students were not achieving, educators in the school reminded formal leaders that the social barriers were too great for them to actually make the kind of difference that the leaders were expecting. And this perpetuated a self-fulfilling cycle of what looked a lot like "learned helplessness" at a school level. Students performed at a low level, educators attributed the performance to a challenging and uncontrollable socioeconomic context while believing they were doing all they could given the circumstances, students continued to struggle, the prevailing educator beliefs were thus reinforced and classroom practice remained the same, and so on and so on. The school garnered a fair number of external resources from the district, but these resources were not focused on teacher professional learning in the service of improved classroom practice. The resources included things like social workers, child and youth counselors, education assistants, a psychologist, community outreach workers, and nutrition assistants, to name just a few.

Recently, a new principal was assigned to the school. His early experiences were similar to those of previous principals. Teachers felt that he needed to understand that this particular school was very unique in light of the challenges the students faced. The principal met very dedicated teachers who wanted to make a positive impact on the lives of their students, but who were clear in their beliefs that the prevailing socioeconomic and mental health challenges that students experienced meant that the grade-level academic expectations were unrealistic and not attainable. The teachers were kind, compassionate, and well-intentioned. When the principal asked questions in order to gain insight into the school, the students, and their learning, the teachers politely worked to "educate" the new principal about "how different things are here." The teachers felt that it was necessary to help him understand the importance of making sure that students were fed each morning and at lunch, for example. They believed that he would soon understand that the challenges students and their families experienced would become the focus of his day. He would come to see that the school did not have enough social work and psychological support to assist these children. And finally, the teachers believed that the principal would soon realize that catering to the very real social needs of students on this scale is a full-time job.

Though the new principal agreed that the challenges in this particular school were real and prevalent, he was not willing to lower his expectations for high-quality teaching practice in each and every classroom. He understood that he would need to spend some of his time ensuring that the social and emotional needs of students were met, but not at the expense of effective instructional practice and enhanced student achievement. The school's lagging student achievement results also meant that it was a primary concern for the area superintendent. The superintendent visited the school often, always with suggestions for how the principal and teachers should help the students achieve. She wanted the principal to act with urgency. She felt that the school had been underperforming for far too long and wanted to know what the principal was going to do about it. And she wanted to know what the principal was going to do to "get" positive student achievement results *quickly.*

(Continued)

(Continued)

The principal understood these expectations and their urgency, but he also knew that he had to develop relationships in the school in order to be able to motivate, guide, facilitate, and support teachers effectively to bring about these positive results. In other words, the urgency for student achievement required time for the principal to work effectively with the teachers. And this temporal tension was wrapped up in the bigger challenge of the prevailing culture of care coming at the expense of a culture of learning. The culture of care wasn't just experienced; it was written down and formalized in the school improvement goal that was guiding the professional learning of staff. The teachers' professional learning efforts were explicitly focused on responding to the social and emotional needs of the children. This isn't a focus that one could (or even should) argue with. The unintended consequence, however, was that the impetus for changing and improving classroom practice was absent. The school improvement goal made no mention about changing instructional practice. But the principal knew that without changes to instruction in classrooms, there would be no improved student learning outcomes. He also understood the importance of focus and alignment in the school, such that any resources that he and the teachers were given to improve instruction would need to be the right ones. He found himself occupying a space in which he needed (and wanted) to build positive relationships with the staff that he had just met, while appreciating the urgent expectations of the superintendent. We'll return to this concrete illustration later. For now, let's zoom back out to the bigger picture as we continue to understand the challenge of leading in the middle space.

IMPLEMENTATION CHALLENGES AT THE NEXUS OF PRESSURES AND SUPPORTS

Let's look a little more closely at this implementation "challenge of practice" that principals face. Principals are expected to lead, and are responsible for, student achievement in their schools. The days of the principal's role being defined exclusively in operational and managerial terms are well behind us in improving school systems (Hattie, 2015; Robinson et al., 2009). Central office personnel are often assigned to support the principal and the school staff in their improvement efforts. Teachers spend most of their day working with their students, and the typical structure of the school day means that large blocks of uninterrupted time for teachers to be working with each other and with the principal are elusive. Even when teachers desire to be very collaborative and look forward to opportunities that will allow them to enhance their practice and extend their learning, the default nature of the day is one that continues to promote a solitary existence.

We know from the research that one of the best ways for a school community to improve student learning is for teachers to de-privatize practice and open their classrooms and their minds to new and varied understandings, perspectives, and behaviors (Katz et al., 2009). Principals play a large part in creating these kinds of professional learning cultures. They know that cultures of professional learning change practices in the service of improved student learning and achievement. At the same time, however, the realities of our current age of (external) accountability mean that central office personnel are simultaneously communicating expectations to schools about how to enhance improvement efforts. Sometimes government resource personnel are sent to some schools and some districts, especially when improvement efforts seem to be particularly challenged. And added to this mix, of course, are teachers who have their own opinions, beliefs, and ideas about how to improve their students' learning; they too bring plenty of experience and expertise into the conversation. The principals' implementation challenge of practice includes coordinating and making sense out of all these differing supports or ideas, especially when coherence among them isn't obvious and the experience is perceived as "clutter" (Fullan & Quinn, 2015). Principals find themselves living (and working) at the nexus of a range of pressures and supports, some internal and some external.

AN IMAGE TO HOLD IN MIND

Let's return to our concrete illustration. After many years of low scores on standardized tests, the school we are talking about had been placed on an official government list of schools that needed to improve. The school district also saw this school as one of its lowest-performing schools. The new principal felt a tension every time he met with his area superintendent because he was given clear direction that improvements needed to be more evident. Further, when centrally assigned instructional coaches worked in the school, they attempted to provide teachers with many different resources and programs that they might use to help their students learn, but without ongoing opportunities to consolidate learning, these interventions did not take hold. Teachers began to feel less confident about their practices, some grew angry in response to this experience, and others grew discouraged and even withdrawn.

The school was a hotbed of activity, and the teachers were always busy. They were busy planning their lessons, supported by various coaches and consultants. They were busy filling out reports and templates about what they were attempting to do in the classroom and how well their students were doing in light of their programs and interventions. They were expected to measure their students' progress in numerous ways, and to report the results to central authorities. They were expected to engage in workshops, meetings, and professional discussions intended to help them improve. They went to book studies, they tried to visit each other's classrooms, and they were expected to bring student work to the table in order to diagnose where students were in terms of their learning, decide on different strategies and interventions that could be used, or determine the impacts that previous decisions were having on students. The principal stood in the middle of all these activities, which he perceived and experienced as pressures. Being on a government list that indicates your school is underperforming is a pressure. Being visited often by central office staff who arrive with their own agendas for improvement is a pressure. Managing the emotional complexities that teachers are experiencing in light of this expectation to improve is a pressure. And working to balance the professional judgment that each individual teacher brings to the conversation while holding firm to the importance of collaborative professional learning can also be a significant pressure. The principal in the elementary school that we have been describing felt all of these pressures.

INITIATIVITIS AND LITERAL LEADERSHIP

Few ideas resonate as much with the principals we work with as the concept we have referred to as "initiativitis" (Katz et al., 2009). Initiativitis is the disease of the initiative. Among the more than 3,500 principals in Leithwood and Azah's (2014) study, number one on their list of recommendations for reducing workload pressures was to significantly reduce the number of new initiatives. These initiatives tend to be described as prescribed programs, interventions, resources, or processes that come with implementation and accountability expectations in the school. Instead of being perceived as helpful to the improvement process, these intended supports (usually put in place by well-intentioned people) are often accused of distracting schools and their staffs from their improvement work. Teachers sometimes complain that they do not have enough time to teach because they are too busy implementing other people's programs. And they may grow frustrated that their professional judgment is not being honored or that their contextual experience is not being considered in the steadfast pursuit of fidelity to the "initiatives." In this environment, *prescription* and *professional judgment* are cast as competitors, with very different cultural connotations. The former manifests in a culture of compliance and surveillance, while the latter becomes about professional freedom and autonomy. And especially germane to the point we have been making here, the principal is caught right in the middle.

In our experience, new principals are especially prone to contagion when it comes to initiativitis because of what might be called "literal leadership." Literal leadership is what happens when principals engage with the above-mentioned external expectations "to the letter" rather than "in the spirit." In many jurisdictions, there are large numbers of new principals. New principals practice literal leadership when they expect teachers in their schools to implement programs they themselves might not really understand, in a rather algorithmic way. An example of literal leadership can often be observed when new principals attend a system meeting with their school superintendent. These principals are trying to learn many complex facets of their role at one time. They listen closely to everything the superintendent says, and in the absence of prior experience, they believe that they have to implement everything they hear, because that's a typical assumption within a hierarchical organization. The meeting with the superintendent usually includes multiple agenda items. These items may include instructional topics in literacy and numeracy, operational issues such as the rollout of a student information system, and a guest speaker talking about how to improve the learning culture in each school. These principals then return to their schools, and at their next staff meetings they replicate this superintendent agenda without necessarily taking into consideration the context of the school and the improvement work that is already happening. Through this literal leadership practice, the information from the central meeting might stifle or overtake the work at the school rather than support it.

In *Intentional Interruption,* we describe the cognitive bias that results in our tendency and desire to present the strongest version of ourselves to the outside world (Katz & Dack, 2013). When we take on new responsibilities, as new principals do, we often have a heightened and anxious desire to show those around us that we are capable of fulfilling those responsibilities effectively, that we deserve to be where we've recently landed. This desire, often subconscious, to show others (and sometimes ourselves) that that we are capable of fulfilling the expectations of the new role, coupled with a lack of experience around the complexities of managing implementation expectations, might influence a new principal to push rule-based compliance in a way that is not helpful. Through experience, principals come to understand the importance of mediating various expectations, buffering their staff from "activity traps" (Katz et al., 2009) that would harm their efforts, and brokering relationships with external sources to learn how best to proceed in the school with a healthy respect for the local context. In other words, over the course of their careers and with the right kinds of experiences, principals move along the continuum from "emergent" to "proficient" in their understandings and practices. Figure 1.3 outlines this sequence. Note the heavy emphasis on "rules" in the early stages; it is this reliance on rules that manifests as literal leadership. Over time, as school leaders move closer to the proficient end of the continuum, they can learn how to fulfill system expectations without being too literal. That is, they can learn how to reconcile local and central positions and move beyond the either/or statements, or perceived polemics (a set of seemingly incompatible alternatives), that characterize much of education.

Figure 1.3   Stages in Growth From Emergent to Proficient

No practical experience. Dependent on rules.	Expects definitive answers. Some recognition of patterns. Limited experience. Still relies on rules.	Analytical. Locates and considers possible patterns. Has internalized the key dimensions so that they are automatic.	Uses analysis and synthesis. Sees the whole rather than aspects. Looks for links and patterns. Adjusts to adapt to the context.	Understands the context. Considers alternatives in an iterative way and integrates ideas into efficient solutions. Solves problems and makes ongoing adaptations automatically.

Source: Earl and Katz (2006b).

POLEMICS IN THE MIDDLE SPACE

In this chapter we have described an implementation challenge of practice for school leaders who are charged with leading school improvement efforts by creating the conditions for impactful professional learning. These leaders occupy a space between the decentralized realities of classroom teachers looking to exercise (and learn through) *bottom-up* professional judgment processes and the centralized efforts of *top-down* prescription. Though both are typically well intentioned, the result is an experiential tension for school leaders. They are pulled between what we call "the knower" (what one already "knows" from one's own beliefs and experiences; in this case, the bottom-up professional judgment) and "the known" (codified knowledge from theory and research; in this case, the top-down prescription) of professional learning and become mired in polemics (Katz, 2000, 2002). In the next chapter, we outline our concept of the intelligent, responsive school as a way of moving beyond the polemics that come from leading in the middle space.

TIME FOR REFLECTION

1. What impact do "top-down" and "bottom-up" pressures have on you, your staff, and your school?

2. Professional learning is at the heart of all school improvement processes. How effective is professional learning in your school, and how do you know?

3. Describe the culture of expectations in your school and the impact this culture has on staff practice and student outcomes.

2

The Intelligent, Responsive School

In Chapter 1 we described the challenge of being a principal occupying the middle space between the decentralized contextual realities of classroom teachers looking to learn through *bottom-up* professional judgment processes and the centralized efforts of *top-down* system prescription. This, we noted, often results in an experiential tension for school leaders as they are pulled between various forms of these dichotomies. The consequence is an argumentative discourse, with principals caught between sets of what feel like "either/or" propositions that are all ultimately supposed to be about enhanced professional learning in the service of student achievement and success. And it becomes easy to lose sight of this core (and agreed-upon) improvement objective as otherwise well-intentioned people get caught up in polemics. In this chapter, we recast the experiential tension as a creative one, and our assertion is that a certain kind of wisdom exists in the space between the perceived incompatibilities—namely, an opportunity for impactful professional learning.

THE POWER OF *AND*

In his recent book *The Achievement Habit* (2015), Stanford professor Bernard Roth explains how our language shapes the way we approach our goals. He argues that the way we speak not only affects how others perceive us but also has the potential to influence our own behavior. Among his suggestions for linguistic "tweaks" that can enhance success is to swap *but* for *and*. He explains that when we use the word *but*, we create a conflict that may not in fact exist, but that our minds (and brains) are forced to reconcile as incompatible in order to deal with the perceived cognitive dissonance (the discomfort we feel when we believe we are holding two contradictory beliefs at the same time). Alternatively, when we use the word *and*, our minds get to consider how we might deal with both parts of the goal or challenge—for example, to have both "prescription" *and* "professional judgment" in our professional learning efforts. At its heart, Roth's approach capitalizes on design thinking; it forces an intentional consideration of otherwise automatic thinking and makes it possible to solve problems and achieve objectives that aren't as incongruous as they might seem. Making a conscious effort to substitute *and* for *but* in our discourse is an intentional interruption!

The design thinking that informs the rationale for the linguistic substitution described above also underscores the work on "integrative thinking," which has been most influential in a business context (Martin, 2007) but is becoming increasingly recognized as an important learning outcome in other situations, including for children in schools. Integrative thinking has taught us that we often *create* situations that set up "either/or" as opposed to "both/and" solutions. We retreat to the poles of our options and argue our positions, even though there are likely valid perspectives in both positions and in every other in between. In his book *The Opposable Mind* (2007), Roger Martin helps us understand that the tension between opposing ideas is never considered a bad thing in integrative thinking. Rather, the integrative thinking model invites us to dive into these opposing positions by articulating what each means, by examining their similarities and differences, by identifying assumptions that may exist around each of them, and by exploring all possibilities in a positive way. Most of us have been taught that when faced with a difficult decision we would do well to create a "pro/con" list. The integrative thinking method challenges this conventional wisdom and instead invites us to create a "pro/pro" list so that both decision paths can be examined together in a way that brings out the best in each and suggests a creative way forward.

Take, as a relevant example, a common and continuously swirling debate in professional learning conversations: Should professional learning be private and self-directed or not? As learners, we do need to own our learning. We do need to ask critical questions about our practices and sort out ways to gain new insights, understand different perspectives, and improve our skills. We know that when we're interested (and motivated) to learn something, we're more likely to do the hard work involved in learning it. Self-direction clearly matters. But at the same time, learning is not an isolated activity. Learning has a social dimension; we collaborate with others to share ideas, offer our perspectives, and hear theirs. We know that critical friendship is a powerful notion (Baskerville & Goldblatt, 2009; Costa & Kallick, 1995; MacBeath, 1998). In the spirit of friendship and support, critical friends help us see what we might be missing, sometimes because we're too close to a situation, and sometimes because we're too sure of ourselves. In *Intentional Interruption* we underscore the essential function that others serve in interrupting the various cognitive biases that preserve and conserve the status quo of our understanding and practices that inhibit real new learning through challenge. People, through the simple fact of being human beings, aren't very good at "choosing" to challenge themselves, and they certainly aren't very good at self-creating the conditions for the dissonance that is an essential prerequisite for new learning (Katz & Dack, 2013).

And so professional learning that's private and self-directed often won't get people across the threshold of challenge that's required for real new learning. We need others to help us. But does the reliance on others—our colleagues—make learning less likely because it undermines our autonomy and self-direction? We think not.

Add to this the value that school systems offer in supporting learning by providing access to research and evidence for learning teams. When a learning team struggles because the members lack information or knowledge, the system (through person or process) can function as a "knowledgeable other" to broker access to the research and evidence that could help the team find a way forward. From an integrated thinking standpoint, it's an "and," not an "instead." Simply put, the motivation (and engagement) that comes from the self-directed desire to learn, coupled with the value added by the perspectives and critical friendship of others and the access to a wider body of knowledge that comes from the system direction, will likely yield the most favorable and impactful result. We need the best of all of it!

PRESCRIPTION *AND* PROFESSIONAL JUDGMENT

In 2010, McKinsey Consulting published an important report titled *How the World's Most Improved School Systems Keep Getting Better* (Mourshed, Chijioke, & Barber, 2010). It consolidates key observations and findings from a global comparative analysis. Improving school systems, it turns out, know how to balance the competing demands of local and system expectations. Improving systems know how to contextualize their interventions by determining to what degree something should be mandated *and* to what extent more subtle forms of persuasion should be used. The report goes on to explain an observed correlational relationship between a system's performance stage and the tightness of central guidance to schools. Improving systems "prescribe" adequacy *and* "unleash" greatness. Notice that it doesn't say they unleash adequacy.

And it also doesn't say they prescribe greatness. It says that what a system does depends on what it needs, and what a system needs is based on where it is in the improvement journey; improving systems know both what to prescribe and how to unleash.

Put slightly differently, improving systems understand that unique sets of interventions need to be employed in order for the systems to get better. They pay attention to both the "what" of the intervention *and* the "how" of implementation. They pay attention to both prescription (in relation to the what) and professional judgment (in relation to the how). We refer to the what as a set of "intelligent expectations." And we refer to the how as "responsive"—responsive to local, contextual peculiarities that are key to effective implementation of the intelligent expectations. The school is where the intelligent and the responsive meet.

INTELLIGENT EXPECTATIONS

We know quite a lot about what works in education. In her Wallace Foundation Distinguished Lecture, Catherine Snow (2015) takes us on a brief history of educational science and reminds us how education has improved over the past 150 years based on things we now know. Things like the fact that we no longer assume that anyone who knows how to read can teach reading, and that we now recognize the value to students of learning in settings where they encounter all kinds of diversity. We know that high-quality early childhood programs staffed by professionals using rich language promote child development, and that classrooms in which authentic discussion occurs regularly are sites of better learning and higher levels of student engagement, to name just a few examples. The What Works Clearinghouse (WWC), an initiative of the U.S. Department of Education's Institute of Education Sciences, was established to provide educators, policy makers, researchers, and the public with a central and trusted source of scientific evidence of what works in education. The name itself makes this mandate clear, and approximately a thousand evidence-based entries now exist in the WWC.

Among the many jurisdictions where we we work, probably no effort to define "what works" has captured the attention of educators more than John Hattie's *Visible Learning* (2009). The *Times Educational Supplement* endorsed the book as revealing "teaching's Holy Grail." A synthesis of more than eight hundred meta-analyses relating to the influences on achievement in school-age students, *Visible Learning* informs educators about the effect sizes (in relation to student learning and achievement) of a multitude of strategies and practices. Some strategies and practices have strong effects on learning, while others have weak, no, or even negative effects. The particulars of what works and how well are beyond the scope of this book, and *Visible Learning* does a masterful job of spelling it all out. For our purposes, the key point is that we would call a school "intelligent" when it strives to use what is already known about what works, and when its teachers are supported to learn these things and to implement them with fidelity.

Prescribing intelligent expectations makes sense to us. Why waste time reinventing the wheel or expending effort on what we already know doesn't work? An intelligent school understands the difference between problems of practice for which there are already evidence-based strategies for moving forward and those that are true adaptive challenges, challenges where the knowledge to move forward doesn't yet exist and needs to be created. (More on the latter when we shift to a consideration of the responsive.) For example, much evidence exists about how to teach students to read and about how to intervene effectively when students are struggling to read. And this evidence has existed for a considerable period of time. The intelligent school would ensure that teachers are properly trained and supported to utilize the strategies and appropriate interventions to ensure student success. This would be considered a "focused approach to instruction," a key property of what Ken Leithwood (2013) defines as a "coherent instructional guidance system," which has been found to be a core dimension of strong school districts. As Leithwood puts it:

> A district's instructional guidance system should be aimed at influencing the use of instructional practices supported by the best available evidence and considerable work has been done . . . to highlight those practices for districts and schools. . . . There is now an emerging, evidence-based consensus about the central features of most forms of powerful instruction. . . . It is these central features that strong districts capture in their instructional guidance systems. (p. 113)

Informed or Uninformed Prescription

Thus far, we've defined the notion of intelligent expectations and we've argued for the value of a prescriptive stance in moving them forward. There's an inherent efficiency in this strategy. After all, does it really make sense for teachers to experiment their way into an understanding about how to teach students to read? Or about how to construct a comprehensive literacy block? Or about any number of the things that currently reside in our various repositories of collective wisdom like the What Works Clearinghouse or *Visible Learning*? People like the idea of being on solid, evidence-based footing as they do their work, yet *prescription* is often imbued with an undesirable quality. In the large range of districts that we work and spend time in, prescription is basically a swear word among school practitioners. It connotes a lack of autonomy, of agency, of free will, and, as we've seen, of respect for professional judgment.

While we've asserted that an integrative thinking approach can help us see value in moving beyond the prescription versus professional judgment polemic (by showing us that they are actually not incompatible), we think that we would do well to reorient attention in the direction of a different polemic, one that we think does a better job of capturing what's at the heart of the perceived incompatibility. The more meaningful distinction in our view is between "uninformed" and "informed." Prescription can be both uninformed and informed (Barber, 2001). Uninformed prescription presents as a dictated direction that has no appeal to a knowledge or evidence base other than perhaps an authority's ideological view. The response to any "why" question in an uninformed prescription scenario—should one be brave enough to ask—is often the same as that a two-year-old gets from a parent who is fed up with noncompliance: Because I said so!

Informed prescription is different. Reasons, in the form of research and evidence, inform and accompany the prescription, with no waiting for someone to ask why. A prescriptive expectation that is uninformed can lead to difficult and damaging outcomes. When educators are told to implement something that is not grounded in evidence and that does not lead to improved outcomes for students, they lose confidence in the source of the directive. And when this happens too many times, they understandably become change averse and potentially weary of prescription. Informed prescription, on the other hand, trades in the currency of evidence-based reasons. The better the reasons, the better the understanding. And the better the understanding, the better the fidelity to implementation. Intelligent schools work within the clear parameters of a focused approach to instruction, relying on informed prescription to make a difference by capitalizing on what's "known" (from research and evidence).

RESPONSIVE CONDITIONS

In many jurisdictions, intelligent expectations take the form of intelligent (and expected) practices. Such instructional and assessment practices include (but are certainly not limited to) things like the importance of defined learning intentions, co-constructing success criteria with students, creating classroom environments that welcome errors, setting challenging/rich learning tasks, and using feedback to close learning gaps (Hattie, 2009). These intelligent and expected practices are often referred to as "high-yield" strategies, and they form the core of many successful districts' coherent instructional guidance systems. That said, we've lost count of the number of schools we've been in where the principal, charged with leading school improvement efforts, says something like "We're doing the high-yield strategies but they're not working!" Here's the thing: what makes these strategies high-yield strategies is the yield. They have to work. We would argue that a high-yield strategy without the yield isn't a high-yield strategy. Perhaps, if we are granted license to be a bit cheeky, the What Works Clearinghouse might be more appropriately labeled the What's *Supposed* to Work Clearinghouse.

We know enough about the real work of knowledge mobilization in education to understand the severe limitations of an approach that legitimates the distinction between knowledge production (i.e., knowing what works) and knowledge application (i.e., getting it to work in the context of real life). Many of education's most pressing problems, to use Snow's (2015) words, live in the no-man's land between basic and applied sciences. She goes on to say that a "disastrous drawback of the traditional basic/applied distinction [has been the assumption] that if the basic science [is] sound, the application process [is] simple, requiring only interpretation or translation" (p. 461). Tony Bryk (2015), in his critical look at the evidence-based practice movement in education over the past decade, offers us a way of understanding this distinction between "what works" and "what's supposed to work." He explains how the randomized clinical trial, the traditional gold standard in research, forms the foundation for defining an intervention as one that works, after which it might be reviewed by the WWC and put on an "approved list." The problem, however, is that this process tells us that some intervention "can" work. That is, if a field trial produces a significant effect size, it means that the intervention worked somewhere for somebody. What we don't know is what it will take to make the intervention work for different subgroups of students and teachers or across a variety of contexts. As Bryk puts it, "The difference is between knowledge that something can work and knowledge of how to actually make it work reliably over diverse contexts and populations" (p. 469). Stated more simply, and germane to our point here, it's a false dichotomy to try to separate *what works* from *how to make it work in variable contexts.* That's how we end up talking about "high-yield strategies" without the "yield"!

Schools and the people who lead and work in them need to learn how to be responsive. A foundational principle of a responsive school is that students are unique and classrooms are diverse. Context matters. A responsive school grapples with challenges that emerge when intelligent expectations and practices don't land as intended. More than simply problems to solve, these challenges of practice become authentic professional learning spaces for teachers (and— particularly important for this book—leaders) to inquire and improve in. Let's return to our earlier example of teaching literacy, something about which the education community at large knows quite a lot. Dale Willows and her team's Balanced Literacy Diet website (http://www.oise.utoronto .ca/balancedliteracydiet) provides a masterful example of what's out there. Through a robust research program, the site defines the "food groups" of a balanced literacy diet and provides "recipes" for teachers to teach students. Intelligent schools employ evidence-based instructional strategies and interventions like these. The strategies and interventions are implemented with fidelity. Many students improve, but some do not. What do educators do then? A responsive school uses this as an opportunity and space for staff to get better. A responsive school understands that teacher learning must connect explicitly to the learning needs of the students in their classrooms who have not been impacted as intended by the intelligent expectations.

In a responsive school, professional learning resources and opportunities focus on the specific and challenging questions that individual teachers have. These questions emerge from teachers' efforts to fulfill the intelligent expectations in the best ways they know how. These questions become the inquiry questions that launch collaborative inquiry professional learning opportunities for practitioners in schools. The specifics of the teacher collaborative inquiry process are beyond the scope of this book, but the key idea of interest here is that responsive schools *create the conditions* for authentic collaborative inquiry that grounds school-based professional learning communities. (For a very practical and comprehensive discussion of collaborative inquiry for teachers, see Jenni Donohoo's *Collaborative Inquiry for Educators,* 2013.)

Because students and staff are different and have different needs, a responsive school honors the systemic and intelligent expectations but realizes that a "one size fits all" approach is antithetical to successful implementation. For example, a principal responding to expectations from the district central office might declare that everyone in the school is working on a certain aspect of literacy instruction or mathematics instruction. The principal may decide that a portion of each staff meeting will be focused on this particular learning and may further direct that any time provided to teachers for collaboration include this topic. What the principal expects, aligned with district expectations, is certainly an important condition for student learning. But what happens if this is not a learning need for every teacher in the school? In light of the urgent and specific student learning needs that are emerging in classrooms, a teacher and his or her learning team might actually need to focus on learning something else. A responsive school ensures that intelligent expectations are being fulfilled but understands that everyone does not necessarily need to learn the same thing to bring about improvement for each and every student.

Psychologists know that engagement is the visible face of motivation, which is an internal state (Woolfolk, Winne, & Perry, 2015). In order for people to remain engaged in their learning, and to work hard at it, the learning needs to be just in time, job embedded, and needs based; in other words, it has to be authentic (Katz & Dack, 2013). Our learning needs are influenced by intelligent expectations, but the responsive nature of our work becomes significant in light of our contextual specificity.

THE RELATIONSHIP BETWEEN INTELLIGENT AND RESPONSIVE

Some educators might struggle to understand how a school can be both intelligent and responsive. Some educators believe that they are the ones responsible for delivering the program to students, that they know best what their students need, and that they don't need to rely on information about instructional practice from someplace else. The notion of "intelligent," for some, connotes prescription, and that, in turn, feels top-down and disrespectful of the professional judgments of educators based on the unique contextual dimensions of their classrooms. On the other hand, other educators might be suspicious of responsive approaches. They might worry that without clear direction, and without processes that ensure that such direction is being implemented, a responsive approach could be chaotic, devoid of standards, and ultimately harmful to student learning. People who subscribe to this view might worry about the absence of quality control that comes with increased variability. They might feel that students could be disadvantaged depending on who their teachers happen to be. And they might feel comforted by the consistency in processes, strategies, and practices that have been identified as effective.

Intelligent expectations that proceed without respect for context can be just as ineffective as responsive efforts that do not respect the evidence-based practices that are intelligent. Earlier in this chapter we suggested that the more meaningful distinction—and the real incompatibility—is between practice that is uninformed and practice that is informed. Recall our distinction between uninformed and informed prescription. "Do it because I said so" is very different from "Do it based on this evidence and for these reasons." The same uninformed/informed distinction can be applied to the responsive stance of professional judgment (Barber, 2001). Uninformed professional judgment says, "I'm a professional so leave me alone to make my own decisions." Informed professional judgment, in contrast, says, "This is my evidence and these are my reasons for doing what I think makes sense." We argue that intelligent and responsive are not orthogonal constructs. They are not contradictory and they are not incompatible, providing that we have the informed varieties of both.

Intelligent and responsive stances interact and need one another. Earlier we pointed out the shortcomings of thinking about knowledge mobilization as a simple exercise of "reach," of getting the knowledge to the user. We have all encountered the myriad of resources that exist to assist teachers with their practice. We have all watched videos, read books, and attended workshops, conferences, and other learning sessions that were supposed to mobilize existing knowledge (intelligent ideas and practices) in ways that would have positive impacts on teacher practice at scale. But they often did not. And then attributions have quickly followed—that teachers are set in their ways, resistant to change, not interested in learning, and so on. Or, alternatively, the conclusion has been reached that we need to figure out how to mobilize existing knowledge in ways that are more useful to teachers. In *Intentional Interruption* we explain the limitations of tackling knowledge mobilization as strictly a supply challenge— by *supply*, we mean providing (or supplying) the right capacity-building resources, be they human or material. Just because knowledge is available doesn't mean that people will need, want, or—most important—use it, regardless of how intelligent it might be. Needing, wanting, and using what's intelligent—what we've called the conditions for "demand"—come most authentically from a responsive space (Katz & Dack, 2013).

For example, in the jurisdiction of our home province of Ontario that includes some five thousand schools and two million students, math instruction and math achievement have caused much concern over the past few years. Researchers have worked to identify the reasons for these problems, instruction has been examined in countless classrooms and schools, and coaches and consultants have spent extensive amounts of time supporting teachers to improve their math instruction in the service of improved math learning outcomes for students. Finding instructional and curricular resources to assist in this improvement effort isn't hard. However, despite the existence of a veritable cornucopia of resources, it would appear that in many circles they aren't used. Leaders have responded by trying to devise plans to make these resources "accessible," in the broadest use of this term. Put differently, the knowledge mobilization response has been one of trying to enhance reach. But what if we consider this challenge from a different perspective, from the vantage point of the intelligent, responsive school? In an intelligent, responsive school, our best efforts at implementing high-quality, "expected" mathematics teaching practices may have achieved variable outcomes in student learning. Shifting into a responsive stance, we would seek to understand why. A learning team might develop some critical questions about why students are struggling with proportional reasoning, for example, and the team members might think about their own practices (and consequent professional learning needs) in that regard to decide where to focus their efforts. This creates a "demand," a need and want to know, that propels them to speak to experts, to access and understand existing research, and to engage with various resources. In an intelligent, responsive environment, knowledge mobilization is less about reach and more about a culture of impactful professional learning that creates the conditions for demand.

Educators' commitment to being responsive as they learn from their efforts to mobilize the intelligent has potential to cycle back around. The way we describe this phenomenon is that today's responsive can be tomorrow's intelligent. The world of classroom assessment has taught us that the best feedback feeds forward. When we learn from responsive efforts across contexts in systematic ways, we begin to draft new intelligent ideas. For example, for decades educators have worked to meet the needs of students who have been diagnosed with various forms of learning disabilities. And it wasn't too long ago that equating a learning disability with a lack of intelligence (in the traditional sense of the word) was fairly prevalent. Schools created segregated programs for students with learning disabilities, and systems sometimes created special schools as well. As time went on and teachers focused their efforts on learning through various challenges of professional practice that were centered on meeting the needs of students with learning disabilities, it started to become clear across a range of contexts (both people and places) that each individual student has a profile of strengths, interests, and needs. And it became clear that this profile forms the foundation for effective instruction and intervention. Depending on the particular disability, students need to learn strategies to learn effectively and successfully, and teachers need to explicitly teach students to use them. We learned that assistive technology could support students with certain learning disabilities in utilizing strategies that allowed them to have access to the learning in the regular learning environment. And we learned that when clarity exists regarding the specific learning disability, the strategies the student needs, and the interventions and assistive technologies that will be employed, the student with a learning disability often learns and succeeds in the regular classroom. Many districts now hold "inclusion" as an intelligent expectation, which has a positive effect on students' social and emotional state. In this example, engaging in responsive professional learning led to changed practice, which now informs intelligent expectations. There is much wisdom to be found in the symbiotic relationship between the intelligent and the responsive. Table 2.1 outlines the foundations of this interaction.

Table 2.1   The Relationship Between Intelligent and Responsive

Intelligent	Responsive
• Clear expectations informed by evidence and research become the parameters for system work. • Clear communication about these directions happens on every level of the organization. • The rationale for implementing certain expectations is understood. • Training is offered to implement what is known, not debate it.	• The creation of clear expectations is informed by multiple learning contexts serving diverse needs. • The voices of educators working with students influence this communication and make it authentic. • The rationale for engaging in an inquiry process to gain new understanding is understood. • Professional learning is influenced by context and the needs of students and staff, which means that aspects of this learning will look and feel different.

BEYOND POLEMICS

In this chapter, we have outlined a preferred future in which the tension between perceived opposites can actually lead to effective learning and improved practice. Consistent with an integrated thinking approach, we have suggested that we gain greater wisdom by looking at the value in all models as opposed to choosing one model with all its strengths and weaknesses over another. When schools are intelligent, they provide clear evidence and research-informed direction to their staff. When schools are responsive, they understand the unique circumstances in each classroom and in each learning team that must be honored so that the learning that emerges from these teams is informed by intelligent expectations but is grounded in the classrooms where the learning teams are responsible for student learning. In the next chapter, we turn to a consideration of what it means to lead in an intelligent, responsive school by engaging in intelligent, responsive leadership practice.

TIME FOR REFLECTION

1. How might you use "both/and" thinking in your school?

2. What are some examples of "informed prescription" and intelligent expectations in your school/district, and what impact do you believe they have on staff and students?

3. What are the critical questions that are guiding professional learning at your school, and how is your school/district being "responsive" to support this professional learning?

3

Intelligent, Responsive Leadership Practice

We have discussed the tension that many principals feel as they mediate between the expectations of teachers in classrooms and the expectations that are coming from the district. And we have outlined a vision of the intelligent, responsive school. Intelligent, responsive schools, however, require intelligent, responsive leadership. In this chapter we will describe what intelligent, responsive leadership practice entails. In subsequent chapters we will describe how to get there—specifically, how to build the necessary skill set to engage in intelligent, responsive leadership in order to exert a positive influence on school improvement.

AN IMAGE TO HOLD IN MIND

Let's return to the story of the principal that we began in Chapter 1. When this new principal arrived at the school and began to understand the staff and the community, he was able to be responsive to the context in which he was now leading. Trained as a facilitator who understood the adult learning process, this new principal spent the first months listening, observing, and asking questions about the experiences educators were having within the school, and how they perceived their students. He was willing to share his own professional questions with his staff, he was not afraid to admit what he didn't know about improving student outcomes, and he invited teachers to engage in a collaborative inquiry process that was different from what these teachers had experienced before. By initiating his work in the school in this way, the principal was able to show his ability to be responsive to his new school community.

You will recall that this particular school was under tremendous scrutiny because of many years of low performance. The principal, working closely with staff, needed to consider the kind of leadership that was required in the school in order to bring about necessary improvements. He also needed to consider the very important problems and concerns that the staff agreed must be addressed for the school to serve its students more effectively. These focus areas would be the foundation for any professional learning that was required. Further, the principal needed to ensure that all of the staff's learning was directly connected to classroom practice and instruction, because he understood that it is only through changes to classroom practice and instruction that student achievement can improve.

Early on in this process, a number of teacher leaders emerged who had always wanted to bring about change in terms of student learning at the school but had not felt that the culture of the school would support their leadership in this regard. By creating supportive conditions for professional learning, the principal began to open the doors for teachers who really wanted to make a difference in terms of student learning. While the initial experience of arriving at an authentic learning focus, engaging in an effective collaborative inquiry process, and sharing leadership across the school was challenging, momentum to engage in this type of work began to increase. The reason for this positive development was that the learning teams in the school began to see the benefits of having a very clear learning focus. They understood the importance of collaborating with one another in order to think differently about their practice. They appreciated the opportunity to try different things in their classrooms and to feel the support of their colleagues throughout the process. Most important, these changes to instructional practice began to have an impact on student learning. Teachers realized that by focusing on their own learning, by changing their attitudes and practice, and by working with their students differently, they could actually bring about student results that had never been experienced in the school before.

These teachers, working with the principal, understood the importance of gathering evidence in this learning process. They wanted evidence to know if they were "getting better" and if they were making a difference for their students. In the past, much of the "evidence" that was being discussed in various meetings consisted of their perceptions about student poverty, student mental health issues, and lack of support from parents. Though these are valid concerns, the focus of their previous discussions was seldom on classroom practice. The evidence that was previously being discussed had very little to do with instruction, the impact this instruction had on their students' achievement, and the ways that instruction might need to change in order to support students more effectively in terms of their learning. By staying focused on their instructional challenges of practice, remaining committed to the collaborative inquiry process, and working closely with the principal to share leadership in order to create an effective learning culture, most of the school staff began to see how their collective effort was making a difference for student achievement. Let's look to the research to better understand how this principal was engaging in intelligent, responsive leadership practices.

LEADERSHIP, PROFESSIONAL LEARNING, AND CLASSROOM PRACTICE

As we've explained elsewhere, important relationships exist among leadership, professional learning, and classroom practice, resulting in improved outcomes for students (Katz & Dack, 2013). A culture of coordinated and shared leadership creates conditions for effective professional learning. Effective professional learning that focuses on classroom practice has the potential to improve teacher practice. And by changing instruction in meaningful ways, teachers have a greater opportunity to improve achievement for all students.

The principal in the school we have been describing in our example understood the importance of school culture. More specifically, he understood that it was important to lead in a way that would influence a culture that had not previously been focused on professional learning that has the goal of leading to necessary changes in classroom practice. Relationship building and trust are key ingredients in impactful professional learning, but instead of spending too much time focusing on these characteristics as *preconditions* to engaging in the learning, the principal helped his staff to build trust, support high expectations, and develop collective efficacy *at the same time* as they were engaging in the work.

AN IMAGE TO HOLD IN MIND

The principal respected the questions that the staff asked. Though he worked with staff to raise the bar on what was expected of the students in the school, he understood that this ideal could be reached only if the staff continued to develop their confidence to meet the needs of each and every student. To that end, the principal worked closely with a leadership team of teachers who volunteered their time to support this learning, with the aim of creating collaborative processes that the staff could use to guide their inquiry. Importantly, in order to be responsive to the context of this particular school, the principal did not ignore the fact that many of the students experienced the challenges of poverty; rather, he worked with the staff to create different ways of providing support for students affected by this very significant issue. He asked the district for support to meet the challenges that this community faced. This support included staff who had expertise in social work and mental health issues. He also asked the district to reach out to other community partners to assist him with finding the right ways to address some of the important concerns that existed in this particular community. He asked those partners to help the educators in the school explore the ways that they could support their students while remaining focused on their core business of teaching and learning. Essentially, the principal invited school staff to focus on the necessary learning without ignoring important issues that they and their students faced each day. If this principal had downplayed some of these challenges, he would likely have been perceived as disconnected from the realities of the community, which in turn could have affected his credibility with teachers, who had been very committed to this particular community for many years. This principal, in collaboration with his staff, understood the context in which they were teaching and leading. Paying attention to important conditions for learning for both staff and students, as well as the context that these educators and students were learning in, the principal and the staff created responsive conditions based on intelligent expectations leading to improvement in student achievement.

One of the best and most comprehensive school leadership resources that we've worked with is the Ontario Leadership Framework—the OLF (Ontario Ministry of Education, 2012). The OLF defines leadership as "the exercise of influence on organizational members and diverse stakeholders towards the identification and achievement of the organization's vision and goals" (p. 3). Further, the OLF describes leadership as being about evidence-based practices as opposed to characteristics. This is an important distinction, because characteristics (such as being inspirational or charismatic) have more to do with the underlying qualities (or traits) that individuals possess. Practices, on the other hand, are those intelligent expectations based on the research that can be enacted in a school and lead to school improvement. Not only is it important to understand what these practices are, but it is also important to understand context in terms of applying them (Leithwood, Day, Sammons, Harris, & Hopkins, 2006). The application of evidence-based leadership practices in local contexts describes the responsive component of the intelligent, responsive school.

INTELLIGENT LEADERSHIP PRACTICES

As we have previously noted, intelligent expectations regarding effective leadership are based on what evidence and research tell us. Responsive leadership means that the way these effective leadership practices are exercised is influenced by local context. Though we will spend some time discussing the "intelligent" practices of leadership in this section, it is essential to underscore the importance of the responsive stance because that's what makes the intelligent practices work. The responsive stance is where leadership as "influence" (as per the OLF definition) takes hold. Without it, the intelligent practices—regardless of how well they're articulated—remain confined to a world of platitudes; they are good for inspirational slogans on mugs and T-shirts, but not much else! As Leithwood, Harris, and Hopkins (2008) state, "The ways in which leaders apply these [intelligent] leadership practices, not the practices themselves, demonstrate responsiveness to, rather than dictation by, the contexts in which they work" (p. 38). How leaders learn to be responsive in enacting the intelligent leadership practices—that is, how they learn to implement through influence—is the subject of Chapters 5 and 6. For now, let's look at what the intelligent practices are.

There is general consensus in the research regarding the significant leadership practices or functions that should be exercised in schools. We use the Ontario Leadership Framework as the categorical organizer for describing them, though we also include related insights from a range of other research literature. As defined by the OLF, the key leadership practices are setting direction, building relationships and developing people, developing the organization, improving the instructional program, and securing accountability. These practices, when effectively enacted, have been shown to have the greatest impact on student learning (Ontario Ministry of Education, 2012).

Setting Direction

Setting direction in a school refers to providing a clear focus and clear expectations for the staff. Researchers have referred to this practice as defining the school's mission (Hallinger, 2005), establishing goals and expectations (Robinson et al., 2009), and establishing and conveying the vision (Hitt & Tucker, 2016). We consider the following to be some of the important characteristics of setting direction:

1. Arriving at focused commitments through a collaborative process that indicates consensus among the staff regarding the challenges to be met in order to improve student achievement in the school (Ontario Ministry of Education, 2012). This process includes facilitating the staff's understanding about their own learning needs in relationship to their students' needs so that clear expectations may be set for the work ahead (Katz & Dack, 2013; Leithwood et al., 2008).

2. Communicating these commitments effectively so that there is a shared understanding across the school (Leithwood, Louis, Anderson, & Wahlstrom, 2004; Robinson et al., 2009).

3. Ensuring that these commitments motivate the staff because they believe that what they are being asked to learn and do is compelling (Leithwood, 2012). Further, leaders understand how important it is to celebrate accomplishments, which leads to additional motivation.

4. Inviting all members of the staff to take responsibility for monitoring the progress toward achieving the goals that have been determined (Leithwood, 2012).

It is important to reiterate that these commitments need to be focused on those instructional practices that are known to make the greatest difference for student achievement. Teaching and learning need to be at the core of this work.

AN IMAGE TO HOLD IN MIND

Let's return to our principal who, with the staff, transformed the learning culture in the school we have described. Setting a clear direction was particularly important in this school, because there were very committed educators working in isolation in their own classrooms, trying to meet the needs of students who possessed many learning challenges. When the staff did come together, they did not have the experience or the tools to engage in collaborative work around their teaching practices. The principal made it clear that the direction the school needed to take was to strengthen the learning culture so as to change instructional practice in order to improve student achievement. He was very open to working with the staff to determine *how* to make this happen, but the expectation to move in this direction was set by him. This is an example where the person who holds positional authority, the principal, has an important role to play, especially when a school community does not understand exactly what it needs to move forward. In order to create a sense of urgency in the school, the principal focused the staff's discussions on how many of the students were unable to read by the end of Grade 1. He compared this percentage of students with the percentages of students who were unable to read by the end of Grade 1 in other schools that had similar demographics. It was hard for the staff to ignore that although other schools were serving students in equally challenging socioeconomic situations, those schools were better able to ensure that students were learning to read.

Another strategy that the principal used to capture the attention of the staff in his early days at the school was to show how students who arrived at this elementary school in kindergarten performed each year all the way through to graduation. In the midst of the many reasons that staff members were giving for troubling student achievement results, the most common explanation was the very high rate of student mobility in (and out of) the school. The principal's strategy of looking at the *same* children from kindergarten through graduation got the teachers to face the fact that many of the students who started in the school in kindergarten and didn't leave actually did not improve very much by graduation. This made it impossible to use mobility as an excuse. An additional troubling note was how many students were invited to leave the regular school program to attend special education classes when they were not able to succeed early in their schooling. The staff had to face the uncomfortable question of "What value are our efforts having on the students who are in our school each day?"

In spite of the efforts described above, a few of the teachers were still trying to hold on to the arguments that their students did not have the appropriate parental support, or that there were mental health issues getting in the way, or that the conditions of poverty simply made it too difficult for the students to succeed. These teachers responded with frustration to the principal's efforts; they felt that he simply did not understand the challenges they all faced, and they further challenged him, saying that he would be hard-pressed to find a school where anyone loved and cared for students as much as this particular staff did. The principal looked at these teachers and respectfully asked, "If our students are unable to read and therefore unable to achieve, how can we say that we are caring for their needs and providing the kind of service that will give them opportunities down the road?" This question struck a chord in most of the staff. The principal succeeded in inviting the staff to the place where they could not ignore that change in instructional practice was required so that student achievement could improve. After "intentionally interrupting the status quo of their thinking" (Katz & Dack, 2013), the principal helped the staff begin the collaborative process that allowed them to arrive at a clear sense of focus, to set a clear direction, to communicate this direction, to motivate each other to work toward achieving the goals of this direction, and to share responsibility for monitoring the impact of their efforts.

Building Relationships and Developing People

The next intelligent leadership practice is building relationships and developing people (Ontario Ministry of Education, 2012). This practice focuses on building capacity with everyone in the school. Robinson et al. (2009) suggest that this capacity is best developed when the principal learns with his or her staff in a climate of relational trust. Hallinger (2005) notes the importance of promoting a positive learning climate in the school, while the OLF stresses the need to encourage a collaborative learning culture. The important aspect of this intelligent leadership practice is that capacity is required to meet challenging goals, and this capacity needs to be created in a culture with high expectations. If capacity is not built in the staff, then the chances of making progress in the "set direction" decrease.

We cannot overemphasize the importance of positive relationships for influencing learning and bringing about important change in a school. A culture that focuses on positive relationships and capacity building prioritizes listening to others and responding equitably, respecting and leveraging the experience and expertise of all members of the staff, and celebrating everyone's accomplishments (Leithwood, 2012). Learning and collaboration are at the center of these positive cultures because everyone in the school knows that it is important to continue learning in order to serve students more effectively, and that by collaborating in particular ways (discussed later in this book), they can achieve wisdom that is much better than the wisdom any one person could create on his or her own. This commitment to continuous improvement includes the understanding that leaders are also learners and that learning happens both in formal settings, like staff meetings, and during informal opportunities, like conversations in staff rooms (Leithwood, 2012; Robinson, Lloyd, & Rowe, 2008).

AN IMAGE TO HOLD IN MIND

After creating a sense of urgency in the school that changes needed to be made in order to improve student achievement, the principal we have been describing understood the importance of creating a positive learning culture and focusing on effective capacity building. As we have mentioned, there were a number of teacher leaders in the school who had not previously felt comfortable coming forward and offering their leadership to support this important learning. With this new sense of urgency, these teacher leaders felt comfortable enough to offer their support. Other notable characteristics of the school were that staff relationships had always been collegial and congenial. Though these characteristics could be a positive foundation for the important learning that needed to happen in the school, they could also be a detriment, because the staff members were more familiar with being *nice* to one another than actually challenging one another in order to improve. We are not advocating for any school community to be uncaring or divisive; however, for real learning to occur there also needs to be a sense of challenge (Katz & Dack, 2013). Because this school community was already a caring one, because the staff had come to terms with the fact that changes needed to happen, and because they understood that learning was a challenging process, they were able to enhance their positive culture through the authentic professional learning that took place there.

Another important relationship-based quality that is often overlooked in schools is that of staff well-being. Leaders speak regularly about student well-being, but they don't often include staff well-being in that discussion. When school staff feel confident, resilient, and capable, an engaging professional learning community emerges. Promoting staff well-being is a way to build relationships and develop people. For example, when teachers believe that they are able to influence the direction of their school, they will be much more willing to contribute their expertise and ideas. When healthy collaboration exists in the school because of a strong sense of trust and positive relationships, chances are that teachers will be more engaged each day in their collective work. When teachers feel affirmed because of the work they are doing and when they experience the impact their work has on students, motivation to continue learning and to improve instructional practice may increase. Because learning can be an uncomfortable process, since it demands that we change (Katz & Dack, 2013), engaging in this learning in a healthy community can support teachers in this endeavor. The principal has a very important role to play in leveraging the expertise of each member of the staff and in enhancing the learning community (Ontario Ministry of Education, 2012). We would argue that professional learning that promotes engagement and leads to more effective practice is an excellent well-being strategy when it unfolds in a learning community that honors each member.

Developing the Organization

Developing the organization is another important intelligent leadership practice (Ontario Ministry of Education, 2012). This practice is about moving beyond specific individuals and focusing on the organization as a whole; it is about transforming the school into a learning organization. Developing the organization is never a static process. New learning has the potential to inform new actions, which leads to continuous improvement. As Hallinger (2005) states, effective principals "are those who have the capacity to motivate teachers to step out beyond the boundaries of their classrooms to work towards the transformation of the school from a workplace into a learning place" (p. 232).

When everyone in the school is working collaboratively to strengthen the learning organization, the school's potential to support student learning increases. These collaborative partnerships don't involve only the staff in the school. School staff also need to partner with parents and community members in order to leverage their expertise and experience to improve student outcomes (Ontario Ministry of Education, 2012). Conceptualizing the school as an organization is important because it is the context that can either support the kinds of improvements we are discussing or actually hinder them. A school's infrastructure, which carries the history and the traditions of a particular learning community, is programmed to perpetuate the status quo in much the same way as individuals do when they subconsciously work to preserve and conserve what they already think, believe, know, and do (Katz & Dack, 2013). Even when teachers realize that change is required, the environment in the school can work against these changes unless all members of the staff pay close attention to the ways in which they may be holding on to previous ways of doing things (Leithwood, 2012).

Because the structures and processes that govern the school are often invisible, the principal has to pay close attention to the actions of the staff, especially when there is a misalignment between what they say they wish to do and what they are actually doing. As we highlighted in Chapter 2, there is plenty of existing research-based evidence to suggest what teachers need to do in classrooms to help students learn better. The important question is, why aren't we doing what we know we need to do in every single classroom? At least part of the answer to this question lies in the fact that the teaching routines and practices that have been used over time have become so automatic that teachers actually think they are implementing something new when they may only be adjusting what they have always done to fit with the language of new ideas (Katz & Dack, 2013; Katz et al., 2009). Developing the organization means that the principal leads teachers in the school to pay very close attention to those things that may not always be visible, and that control the work and the learning in the school. Committing to collaborative processes that lead to effective learning creates an opportunity to challenge some of these invisible processes and structures as they emerge. Dealing with any misalignment between what staff say they want to do and what they are actually doing becomes part of the work. As Leithwood (2012) states, "A school infrastructure misaligned with the practices considered desirable by the school significantly erodes the motivation the staff has to implement those practices and stands in the way of staff making the best use of their expertise" (p. 21).

Leading an intelligent, responsive school means that the principal is always paying attention to what is happening in classrooms throughout the school. Through the collaborative processes in which they participate, teachers have the opportunity to challenge any preconceived notions or invisible structures and processes that may actually be hampering the school's ability to move forward. The principal, in turn, also looks for support from his or her own learning team (discussed in detail in Chapters 5 and 6), so that colleagues acting as critical friends can assist the principal when he or she has become blind to practices that are hindering the ability to learn and to improve.

AN IMAGE TO HOLD IN MIND

The principal we have been describing in our example was part of an effective principal learning team whose members understood how to support each other in terms of leading a school toward permanent change in attitude and action through effective professional learning. His efforts, taken together, made the school "feel" like a different place overall—a place of learning for both adults and children—regardless of the particular individuals who happened to be in the building at any given point in time.

Improving the Instructional Program

Improving the instructional program (Ontario Ministry of Education, 2012) is about planning, coordinating, and developing teaching and learning in a school where administrative

decisions are informed by what we know about effective pedagogy (Robinson et al., 2009). Because teaching and learning are
the school's most important priority, Hallinger (2005) argues, it
is essential for the principal to be "hip deep" in the instructional
program. It is impossible to have an impact on the instructional
program without influencing the professional learning conditions in the school. One of the most important elements of
improving the instructional program involves assisting educators in using data to understand student progress. It is not just
about understanding where a student is on the continuum of
learning—it's also important to understand what the data say
about what teachers need to do to move that particular student
forward (Earl & Katz, 2006b).

Supporting teachers through the collaborative inquiry
process is a powerful vehicle for improving the instructional
program (Donohoo & Velasco, 2016). Sometimes this learning
is school-wide if it becomes clear that an entire staff needs
support in a certain area of practice, while at other times this
support is very individualized, based on the unique learning
needs of a particular teacher. Improving the instructional program also means that there is some stability on staff, so that as
teachers learn together with their principal, they can continue
to deepen their practice in a context that supports this type of
inquiry. Some of the reasons that skilled and experienced
teachers remain in a school are that there are ample opportunities for professional development, leadership is widely
shared and coordinated, time is scheduled for collaboration
and planning, there is a vision that supports instruction, and
trust abounds (Ontario Ministry of Education, 2012).

An additional element connected to improving the instructional program involves the alignment of resources with the
agreed-upon focus areas in terms of teaching and learning
(Ontario Ministry of Education, 2012). A common problem in
many schools is the desire to commit to too many things. The
work in schools is very complex, and in light of all the
improvements educators may wish to make in a school, a
school's improvement plan might be filled with a very long
list of desired outcomes. Earlier, we discussed the importance

of setting direction in a school, a direction that everyone can agree is most important because it is needs based. That said, many improvement plans try to include too many commitments, which makes the process complicated and unwieldy. These multiple commitments do not assist the staff in remaining focused, learning deeply, shifting their practice, and reflecting on impact in terms of student learning. Improving the instructional program demands this level of focus. Aligning finite human and material resources to this focused learning is paramount. And it is crucial to ensure that the area of focus for teaching and learning is based on evidence of what's effective (Hattie, 2009; Robinson et al., 2009).

Robinson and her colleagues (2008) state, "The more leaders focus their relationships, their work, and their learning on the core business of teaching and learning, the greater their influence on student outcomes" (p. 636). Focus is necessary because the school environment requires teachers and principals to accomplish many things, a reality that might inadvertently communicate that everything is equally important. Managing the instructional program is an intelligent leadership practice that is very much aligned with the other leadership practices that we have described. By setting direction, building capacity so that this direction can be realized, ensuring that the organizational conditions support this direction, and never losing sight of the importance of quality instruction for changing outcomes, leaders add value to the school improvement enterprise through their influence.

AN IMAGE TO HOLD IN MIND

Returning to our school example, the principal understood that improving the instructional program needed to be the priority for staff learning. Many of the students came to kindergarten without some of the oral language or early literacy skills required to be successful in school. The teachers in the school were very concerned about this lack of preparation. And, as we've mentioned, the same teachers used a deficit lens to explain why their students were not able to learn to read. They spoke often about how their students did not experience the types of opportunities in their homes and in their communities that supported early literacy and oral language development. Even though many of their students could not read by Grade 2, the focus did not often turn toward the kind of instruction that would help these students learn more effectively or the types of interventions that were required when students were not able to grasp the concepts in the first place. By focusing almost exclusively on what they believed families needed to do to help students learn, the teachers were inadvertently minimizing the impact that they themselves could have through effective instruction.

In this particular school, the professional learning process led by the principal revealed that the teachers were not confident in delivering a balanced literacy program. They were not particularly knowledgeable about the importance of oral language development in the early grades, and they did not feel competent in providing instruction that took into account all the different developmental levels of the students in their classes. Although many of these teachers had been "taught" how to teach students to read, this instruction may not have taken into account the previous experiences the students may have had, nor were these teachers very comfortable knowing what to do when the strategies they were using did not help students read. In order to support the staff's learning by aligning resources, the principal asked the district to assign a literacy coach who had expertise in oral language development. A speech and language pathologist from the district also worked as an expert model directly in teachers' classrooms, so that together they could assist students with oral language development. By engaging in learning about oral language development and early literacy acquisition, the teachers became more comfortable asking their students open-ended questions to capture their interest and invite the students to speak about their experiences. By sparking students' interest, by assisting them to think about things more deeply, and by inviting them to share their

(Continued)

(Continued)

thoughts with others in the classroom, these teachers began to see how quickly their students were able to improve. Though some of the students needed more time to increase their vocabularies and articulate their thoughts and reflections, these teachers came to understand that the learning opportunities they were inviting their students to engage in could actually enhance this development. Many of these teachers had previously used more traditional literacy programs that relied on worksheets to teach various aspects of literacy. Unfortunately, these programs did not necessarily spark the interest of students and lead to deeper thinking and enhanced oral expression. The "worksheet strategy" needed to be replaced by rich dialogue in the classroom, supported by a teacher who knew how to probe students to communicate effectively.

The principal and the teachers understood that the instructional program offered the most impactful way to improve student learning. The teachers in the school needed to accept the context that their students were living in, but not be bound by it. By understanding the impact of effective instruction, and knowing how to intervene with different strategies when learning didn't happen easily for some students, these teachers were able to build momentum for their own learning. In this particular example, by understanding the power of oral language development in the early years, teachers realized that they could change the trajectory of student learning through the way in which they engaged their students in their first years of school, no matter what experiences the students had before. This realization, coupled with the associated changes to classroom practice, brought about a very different outcome for these students.

Securing Accountability

Because public education is funded by taxpayers, it is important that the impact it has on students is both effective and demonstrable. Public confidence is required for there to be continued investment in the important work of teaching and learning, so that students can continue to be well served in our public schools. In light of this context, the Ontario Leadership Framework sets out securing accountability as an additional intelligent leadership practice.

There are many ways to build public confidence in public education. This confidence starts with each student having a positive experience in his or her school. It is enhanced when the teacher and the principal work effectively with the student's family to solve any problems that arise for the child in the school. This confidence increases when it is evident that the child is learning in school and that each year his or her learning improves, regardless of who the child's particular teacher happens to be. And ideally, this child and his or her family experience a learning environment that appropriately challenges the student, provides interventions when the student needs additional supports for learning, and offers learning opportunities that are creative and engaging en route to enhanced skills and understanding for the student. When this is the collective experience of a group of students in the school, that school becomes known for its effective practice and its dynamic learning community. We believe that every school can have this experience and this reputation.

Though the principal is the visible formal leader in the school, and most families would turn to the principal if they have concerns about the quality of the education in a particular school, the type of accountability that we are discussing here asks that *every member of the school community takes responsibility* for creating these conditions. As Richard Elmore (2004) states, "Schools build capacity by generating internal accountability, greater agreement and coherence on expectations for teachers and students, and then by working their way through problems of instructional practice and ever increasing levels of complexity and demand" (p. 254).

The intelligent leadership practices we have been discussing can lead to enhanced accountability. When there is a clear direction in a school that is communicated widely, and when the learning, the relationships, and the organizational conditions support this direction, school staff can explicitly show how their efforts are bringing about positive change. In other words, the intelligent leadership practices are all interrelated, and when these leadership practices are successfully enacted in a school, accountability can increase.

AN IMAGE TO HOLD IN MIND

The school that we have been describing did not have a great reputation in the community. In fact, many families chose to send their children to other public schools outside their immediate neighborhood. The reputation narrative existed because this particular school scored poorly on standardized tests for many years in a row. It had a high suspension rate and a poor attendance history for many students, and it was perceived to be in a part of town where it was not safe for students to live or to go to school. As we have discussed, some of the teachers did not believe that these students would ever achieve success based on their view that the students were not supported at home in ways that would allow them to be successful at school. The teachers spent many hours managing student discipline and trying to engage parents. Many of the parents had had negative experiences when they themselves were in school and were not very willing to participate when called.

As previously described, before the new principal arrived, teaching and learning were seldom the focus for staff discussion, and the fact that the school had a larger special education population than other schools, as well as fewer students reading at grade level, did not seem to cause any great concern within the school. However, the new principal was able to gain the teachers' attention and respect, and they agreed that they had an urgent problem. He was able to begin shifting their views. Teacher leadership began to increase in the school, resulting in shared leadership and a culture of collaboration. Through his willingness to share his own professional questions, the principal began to model an environment that was safe for teachers to learn in. He assisted the teachers in finding a learning focus, building capacity around that focus, supporting that focus organizationally, and reflecting

on its impact on student learning. Over time, high expectations began to be held for each and every student in the school.
Teachers believed that together they could find solutions to most
instructional problems that existed. Through collaborative inquiry,
instructional practice began to change in a way that improved
student learning. Needless to say, these improvements, supported
by the entire staff, began to change the reputation of the school.
Students' reading improved, fewer students were placed in special
education classes, attendance improved, and student discipline
issues decreased. Though the principal played a significant role
in leading this change process, it was clear that everyone in the
school took responsibility for the work that needed to happen.

LEADING AN INTELLIGENT, RESPONSIVE SCHOOL

Leading an intelligent, responsive school means that leaders influence others in the school community by enacting the
intelligent leadership practices described above in ways that
are shaped and informed by the context of the school. For
example, when the new principal we have been describing
arrived at his school, he did not observe a school culture that
focused on learning, emphasized the importance of instruction, or shared responsibility for getting better. He met a
staff that was very committed to the school's students but
was more concerned with their social and emotional needs
than with helping them achieve. Because most educators do
wish to make a difference for their students in terms of their
learning, with the proper direction this school began a professional learning journey that led to changes in instructional
practice that supported improvement in student achievement.
By focusing on implementing the intelligent leadership practices in responsive ways, this principal "influenced" a school
transformation. The school became one that was seen as meeting the needs of its students, with a staff that was willing to
engage students' families and their communities as important partners and to learn continuously in order to improve

instructional practice. All of these efforts led to better student outcomes, something that this staff did not previously see as possible. However, once these improvements became obvious, this success motivated even more effective learning, leading to even more effective practice and, in turn, even better student outcomes.

The leadership practices that we have described in this chapter are intelligent ones, practices that are informed by research and that need to be enacted in each and every school. However, successful enactment—or what allows for the intelligent practices to create the conditions for influence according to their advertised potential—requires contextual responsiveness. As Leithwood (2012) notes, "Judging a leader's development entails not only assessing the extent to which a person is generally skilled in the use of leadership practices, it also entails judging the extent to which they are able to enact these practices in a contextually appropriate way" (p. 13). In our example school, the principal understood that the context he was inheriting was one in which many outside facilitators attempted to tell the staff how to teach. Teachers were expected to produce loads of paperwork as a way to exhibit a certain kind of accountability, to demonstrate that they were "learning" everything the outside facilitators expected. The staff's confidence level was low and the skepticism was high, because this staff felt that outsiders did not understand the challenging socioeconomic context in which the students were living and expected to learn. The new principal had to think about this context when determining how to set direction in a collaborative way, build capacity in the staff through healthy relationships, create the right organizational conditions for success, and focus on instruction that would lead to better outcomes. Knowing the effective leadership practices alone is not enough. Building a deep understanding of *how* to enact these leadership practices in particular contexts in order to influence improvement is where the real work (and professional learning) for leaders lies. In the remainder of this book, we focus on what's involved in getting there.

TIME FOR REFLECTION

1. How do you enact the intelligent leadership practices described in this chapter in your own context?

2. How do the professionals within your school work beyond the walls of the classroom to build an effective learning organization, and what might you need to learn as a leader to make this even better?

3. How are the professional learning processes in your school influencing the setting of direction, the strengthening of relationships, and the improvement of student outcomes?

4

The Psychological Foundations of "Getting Better"

In Chapter 3, we explicated the intelligent practices of leadership and defined what it means to lead intelligent, responsive schools through "influence." In Chapters 5 and 6, we will explain *how* leaders go about building the requisite capacities to lead effectively through influence—in other words, how leaders learn to enact the intelligent practices in responsive ways. Specifically, we will outline the Leader Learning Team (LLT) structure and process that we have developed and refined with the support of numerous school districts over the past fifteen years. In Chapter 5, we will describe how adaptive challenges around the notion of "leadership as influence" are transformed into investigable leadership inquiry questions. In Chapter 6, we will highlight how groups of administrators engage in highly structured "critical friend" interactions to enable true professional learning in themselves and others.

The LLT structure and process that we have developed and continuously refined over the years is research based. We have developed our inquiry-driven capacity-building process for leaders (described in Chapter 5) based on what the research says about what it takes to achieve real expertise. And we have developed our collaborative process for taking up these inquiries (described in Chapter 6) based on what the research says about impactful collaboration. In this chapter, we explicate this research base by describing the psychological foundations of our LLT structure and process, which will be articulated in detail in the next two chapters. Understanding the relevant psychology is central because, as we will see later, structures and processes travel much more readily than their conceptual underpinnings. But it's an understanding of the conceptual underpinnings that is key to effective implementation. Thus, in the first half of this chapter we describe the psychological underpinnings of engaging in leadership learning inquiries (fully articulated in Chapter 5) for the purposes of "getting better." In the second half of the chapter, we describes the psychological underpinnings of the *group* component of the LLT (fully articulated in Chapter 6)—in other words, how the group adds value to the learning and work of the individual.

THE PSYCHOLOGICAL FOUNDATIONS OF LEADERSHIP LEARNING INQUIRIES

John Hattie's (2015) recent research has shown that school leaders who believe that their major role is to evaluate their impact are among the most effective in terms of improved student outcomes. Hattie has also found that leaders who encourage everyone in the school to work together to know and evaluate their own impact are among the most effective. These findings suggest that leaders who consider it a core professional responsibility to *know* the impact of both themselves and others have a significant effect on student learning outcomes. This culture of evaluating impact, where both leaders and teachers are regularly asking the question of whether they are making a difference, starts at the top. When leaders have the mindset of wanting to know the impact they are having, even if it's not always positive, other practitioners are encouraged to want to do the same. We believe that the link between this culture of "know thy impact" (Hattie, 2009) and improved student outcomes occurs because of a corresponding desire to improve in places where the intended impact is falling short.

Those asking the question about impact have an inquiry habit of mind, whereby they are constantly collecting and interpreting evidence in order to be able to advance their understanding of themselves and make decisions to create a better future. As Earl and Katz (2006b) write, an inquiry habit of mind is about leaders "being in charge of their own destiny, always needing to know more, and creating or locating the knowledge that will be useful to them along the way" (p. 18). Asking questions about his or her own impact allows a leader to use that feedback to plan future actions to close any gaps. Very often, we focus our efforts exclusively on measuring the ultimate *outcomes*, or "trailing indicators" (like student achievement), when we would do well to focus on the quality and efficacy of our strategies and practices (the "leading indicators") that fall squarely within our realm of control (McChesney, Covey, & Huling, 2012). An inquiry-minded leader who is regularly evaluating his or her impact is taking the time to learn how to make a difference through the leading indicators, coming up with new and more impactful strategies. In our view, this is why the "know thy impact" culture is related to improved outcomes for students—because leaders and teachers who are evaluating impact are also the ones working to improve, and it is these improvements in school and classroom practices that lead to improved outcomes for students.

Essentially, evaluating impact isn't just about asking "How am I doing?" Rather, it is about asking "How am I doing?" *and* "How can I get better?" It's about a desire to improve. This motivation to want to improve continuously is critical because recent research has shown that regular improvement, in any skill area, is by no means a given (see Ericsson & Pool, 2016). People tend to approach learning a skill by beginning with a general idea of what they are looking to learn, getting some instruction in the skill, practicing until they reach an acceptable level of performance, and then letting the skill become automatic. But at this point, people often make a faulty assumption. We tend to assume that we will continue improving at the skill as a result of simply continuing to do it, when research has shown that this is actually not the case. "Research has shown that, generally speaking, once a person reaches that level of acceptable performance and automaticity, the additional years of practice don't lead to improvement. If anything, the doctor or the teacher or the driver who's been at it for 20 years is likely to be a bit worse than the one who's been doing it for only five, and the reason is that these automated abilities gradually deteriorate in the absence of deliberate efforts to improve" (Ericsson & Pool, 2016, p. 13). Importantly, we don't improve as a result of just doing things over and over again; we need to work on improvement in an intentional way!

Improvement, then, does not happen automatically, but requires "purposeful practice" (Ericsson & Pool, 2016). School leaders who are improvement oriented aren't just practicing what they are already good at. Rather, they tackle what they are struggling with in a very deliberate way. We describe this notion of purposeful practice in the following section. We highlight instructional leadership as an area that requires continual improvement and describe why "naive practice" won't get leaders into that space. We then describe the elements of purposeful practice that make it different from naive practice. Together, these ideas provide the conceptual backbone of the improvement-oriented leadership inquiry process that we explicate in detail in Chapter 5.

The Power of Purposeful Practice

Earlier we alluded to the popular but erroneous belief that the more you do something the better you will get at it—that repeating a skill over and over again, sometimes over many years, will improve performance. This is known as naive practice.

Purposeful practice is significantly different from naive practice in that it is about improving in a focused area, where there are clear goals and a specific plan about how to reach the goals and how to monitor progress (Ericsson & Pool, 2016). As we will see below, purposeful practice is not easy. It is effortful and requires going outside one's comfort zone. When people who want to improve learn what is involved in purposeful practice, they can sometimes feel overwhelmed. That's why it is important to remember that we don't apply purposeful practice—or even need it—in everything. There are many areas in our lives where being "good enough" is truly good enough! In most areas of life we're perfectly fine with being adequate. Purposeful practice is meant for the places where we're not. A tennis player looking to become expert in the sport, for example, is likely fine with being good enough at golf, crossword puzzles, and maybe even his day job (let's just hope that person doesn't work with us!). Tennis is the arena in which he has committed to getting better. It's the place where he is motivated to work hard by going outside his comfort zone, setting specific goals, planning how to achieve them, and determining how progress will be monitored.

Importantly, when it comes to school leaders, being good enough works fine in certain areas. A principal probably doesn't need to be better than good enough at certain operational aspects of the job, such as timetabling. But when it comes to instructional leadership, good enough is not enough. There is too much high-quality evidence that speaks to the impact of instructional leadership on outcomes for students.

According to Robinson et al. (2008), instructional leaders focus their efforts on instructional issues and on teachers' impact on student learning. Instructional leaders are concerned with conducting classroom observations, ensuring that professional development enhances student learning, communicating high academic standards, and making sure that school environments are conducive to learning. For instructional leaders, the focus is on ensuring high-quality teaching that has an impact on student learning.

Extensive research has shown the relationship between instructional leadership practices and classroom instruction, demonstrating the positive impact of instructional leadership and the negative impact of a lack thereof (e.g., Alig-Mielcarek, 2003; Blase & Blase, 1998; Larson-Knight, 2000). At the same time, we are well aware of the robust relationship between classroom instruction and student achievement, with the multitude of findings highlighting that the quality of classroom instruction is the most significant predictor of student learning and achievement (e.g., Darling-Hammond, 2000; Hattie, 2009; Marzano, Pickering, & Pollock, 2001; Nye, Konstantopoulos, & Hedges, 2004). The link between instructional leadership and improved student outcomes, while not always direct, occurs because instructional leadership predicts improved classroom teaching, and improved classroom teaching predicts improved student outcomes.

Given the convincing research base, it is apparent why being good enough at instructional leadership practice is not enough. And, as we have explained, leaders cannot make the assumption that once they've learned something about instructional leadership and continue to practice it, they will continue to improve. Some may assume that simply accumulating more hours of practice, based on years in a job, will naturally lead to improvement. Many are familiar with "the 10,000-hour rule," put forward by Malcolm Gladwell in his well-known book *Outliers* (2008). Essentially, Gladwell asserts that to become an expert in a particular field, one must accumulate 10,000 hours of practice. This "rule" is based on Ericsson, Krampe, and Tesch-Römer's famous study on expertise, published in 1993, which revealed that expert violinists had accumulated many thousands of hours of deliberate practice prior to being considered experts. Among other figures cited in the study, Ericsson et al. found that the best violinists had accumulated, on average, 10,000 hours of practice by age twenty. In *Outliers*, Gladwell summarizes Ericsson et al.'s research, as well as the work of others in the expertise field, by making clear that there is no way an individual can become an expert in any field without exerting a huge amount of effort over many, many years. As Gladwell states, "The idea that excellence at performing a complex task requires a critical minimum level of practice surfaces again and again in studies of expertise. In fact, researchers have settled on what they believe is the number for true expertise: ten thousand hours" (pp. 39–40). However, Gladwell's "10,000-hour rule" appears to be an oversimplification of the research.

The 10,000-hour rule is problematic in a few ways (Ericsson & Pool, 2016). First, there was nothing magical about the 10,000-hour figure in Ericsson et al.'s (1993) study. As mentioned, these researchers cited 10,000 hours as the average number of hours of practice that the best violinists had put in by the time they were age twenty, but an average means that some had put in less practice and some had put in more. In addition, in other domains, the number of hours required to reach a particular level of mastery might vary significantly among individuals. More important to the present argument, however, is that Gladwell does not distinguish between naive practice and purposeful practice in the way that Ericsson and Pool do. As mentioned above, according to Ericsson and Pool (2016), 10,000 hours of naive practice won't get someone to expertise, because without specific, deliberate efforts to improve using purposeful practice (explained in detail below), there is no reason to expect significant improvement to occur. Getting back to the school leader "practicing" instructional leadership over multiple years, there is no reason to expect that naive practice, rather than purposeful practice, will lead to improvement.

Purposeful practice is focused, goal driven, and designed to improve a particular area of weakness. It forces a person to go outside his or her comfort zone to make these improvements. For the tennis player, it might be choosing a particular shot to focus on, one the player has been struggling with, and repeating a drill for a period of time, making changes along the way based on feedback (such as where the ball is landing). For the violinist, it might be hours of practicing scales, focusing on appropriate finger placement and movement, again making changes along the way based on feedback (such as how the notes sound). For the instructional leader, it might be intentional efforts to script and ask more coaching-type questions at a meeting of the divisional professional learning community in order to enable more authentic discourse, again adjusting accordingly (based on how teachers respond). Like athletes and musicians, instructional leaders who engage in purposeful practice go outside their comfort zones, use focused, goal-driven activity to improve an area of weakness, and make changes based on feedback received. How instructional leaders can undertake this kind of purposeful practice is the focus of Chapter 5.

So how is purposeful practice qualitatively different from naive practice? Before we can answer this question, it is important first to address what getting better (or improving) really means from a psychological perspective.

Deep Understanding: The DNA of "Getting Better"

Improving is about developing a more sophisticated mental representation of the area in which one is hoping to get better (Ericsson & Pool, 2016). Years ago, Jean Piaget (1952) described "schemas," the building blocks of human beings' mental models of the world. According to Piaget, schemas—which are units of knowledge, each relating to an aspect of the world—are ways of organizing knowledge. As children, we start out with fairly basic schemas (of objects, people, behavior, ideas, and so on), and as we gain experience with the world, our schemas become more complex. We are constantly changing and adding to our schemas, based on our experiences with the world around us. A young child's schema of "school," for example, may be fairly basic. It might include things like what the building looks like (perhaps she only knows of one school), some friends there, a teacher or two, and the feelings she has about it. As that child grows older, she uses the experiences she has had with school to revise the schema to include more complex ideas, such as the differences between particular schools, various individuals associated with a school experience, relevant emotions, and content or skills she has learned.

And by the time she is an adult, her schema of school is even more complex. We can think of a parallel example using an abstract idea such as love. It is easy think about how one's schema of love becomes more complex as experiences with the world and others within it increase.

As human beings, we have brains that store thousands and thousands of schemas, and we use them, as needed, to interpret and respond to the world around us. When it comes to expertise, the hypothesis is that the schemas of experts (in relation to their areas of expertise) are different and more sophisticated than those of novices. This sophistication of schemas, or mental representations, allows experts to recognize patterns in situations that might seem random to others, resulting in more effective problem solving (Nokes, Schunn, & Chi, 2010). Essentially, having a *deep understanding* of a particular area allows experts more precision in responding to challenges, as well as more flexibility in thinking, which results in more effective solutions. Simply put, deep understanding is the DNA of getting better.

Getting better, then, is about developing more complex and sophisticated schemas or mental representations. Research has shown that the way to build and strengthen mental representations is through a learning cycle of trying something, failing at it, revising the strategy, trying again, and so on (see, e.g., Ericsson & Pool, 2016). We will see that this is an important aspect of our leadership inquiry capacity-building model, described in Chapter 5. Purposeful practice is the cyclical process by which people develop more complex and sophisticated schemas or mental representations on the road to improvement.

The Essential Elements of Purposeful Practice

According to Ericsson and Pool (2016), purposeful practice includes four elements that set it apart from naive practice: specific goals, focus, feedback, and discomfort.

Specific Goals

First, purposeful practice has well-defined, specific goals. Goals are the outcomes or attainments that an individual is looking to accomplish, based on the discrepancy between a current state of affairs and an ideal state of affairs (Woolfolk et al., 2015). Research has shown that setting specific, as opposed to generic, goals improves performance for four main reasons (Locke & Lathan, 2002):

1. *Goals direct attention to the task at hand (and away from distractions).* For example, if our mind wanders while we're working on something, remembering the goal brings our attention back to the task.

2. *Goals mobilize effort.* Having a goal makes us work harder. The more challenging the goal, the more effort we put in (with the caveat that if the goal is too difficult and out of reach, motivation could be reduced).

3. *Goals increase persistence.* We're less likely to give up when we have a specific goal we are looking to reach.

4. *Goals promote the development of new strategies when current ones aren't working.* If we can see that our current strategy isn't contributing to progress toward our goal, we are likely to devise a new strategy to get there.

Importantly, there is a difference between a long-term goal and a well-defined, specific, shorter-term goal that can be used for individual practice sessions. For example, a runner might have a long-term goal of decreasing her marathon running time by thirty minutes, but that isn't a good goal for an individual practice session because it's too far out of reach. The idea is to develop smaller goals, each with a realistic expectation, by making a plan in terms of what exactly needs to happen for the longer-term goal to be achieved (Ericsson & Pool, 2016). The marathon runner might want to cut approximately one minute from each mile in the marathon, but even this is too out of reach as a place to begin. It still needs to be broken down into multiple smaller goals, and the runner will have to choose one to begin with, with a plan for how to make it happen. For example, she may begin with a first goal of cutting thirty seconds off of each of the first three miles of her run. Once she has set the first goal, she needs to figure out how she will approach it. She may, for example, approach this smaller goal by focusing on landing her steps on the middle of her feet rather than on her heels. And so her first goal might be to be able to run her first three miles slightly faster by practicing her foot placement. Purposeful practice is about putting baby steps together to reach a longer-term goal.

We've found that intentionally working toward a learning goal in discrete small steps is a powerful strategy for educational leaders, mainly because of the underlying psychology—what's known as the psychology of "small wins." Working on one small step at a time allows people to experience small wins. A large body of research has shown that small wins have enormous power, and an influence disproportionate to the accomplishments of the overarching victories themselves. As Duhigg (2012) explains: "Small wins are a steady application of a small advantage. Once a small win has been accomplished, forces are set in motion that favor another small win. Smalls wins fuel transformative changes by leveraging tiny advantages into patterns that convince people that bigger achievements are within reach" (p. 112). What this suggests is that working on one small step at a time builds momentum in working toward a goal.

Focus

Purposeful practice is also focused. It is difficult to improve at anything without giving it one's complete attention (Ericsson & Pool, 2016). This is easy to say, but in practice it's hard to do. The research on attention shows that it is both limited and selective (Woolfolk et al., 2015). At all times we have information coming to us from our five senses—what we are seeing, hearing, feeling, smelling, and tasting. We can't possibly pay attention to everything coming in through our senses at once, so we have to select our priorities. While reading, for example, if we attempt to focus on every sensory experience, including the way the chair feels, the light in the room, and the sounds in the background, we will probably have difficulty processing what we are reading. We learn to filter out most of that in order to pay attention to what really matters. In short, attention is a limited resource. For purposeful practice to work, we need to learn to focus our attention. Because focus and concentration are crucial to improvement yet difficult to maintain for long periods, shorter practice sessions with clear goals are more effective than longer ones (Ericsson & Pool, 2016). More frequent and shorter practice sessions often give more "bang for the buck."

Feedback

The third element of purposeful practice is feedback. People have to know how close they are to the goals they are currently trying to reach, and if they're not making progress, what's going wrong (Ericsson & Pool, 2016). If our marathon runner sets a short-term goal of cutting thirty seconds off each of her first three miles, but then she doesn't time herself to know how she's doing, the exercise is moot. Hattie and Timperley (2007) describe feedback as information provided by an agent (either a person or an experience) about an aspect of one's performance or understanding. According to these authors, effective feedback needs to answer three questions: Where am I going? (the goals), How am I going? (the progress being made toward the goals), and Where to next? (what needs to be done to get better). It's the third question that underscores the notion that the best feedback *feeds forward.*

There is a connection between breaking down a goal into small steps (or potential wins, as discussed above) and this idea of feedback. To get the kind of meaningful feedback that tells you how close you are to your goal and what you need to try next to get closer, you must constantly monitor your progress. We find ongoing monitoring to be one of the most elusive capacities in improvement efforts within the education domain. In fact, our home jurisdiction of Ontario, Canada, has named System Implementation and Monitoring (SIM) as a core leadership capacity-building initiative. In our experience, well-intended monitoring efforts often fail to get off the ground because the target goals are too big. The larger and more multifaceted the goal, the more difficult it is to monitor progress. And the more difficult it is to monitor progress, the less likely we are to actually do the monitoring. In other words, our "motivation to monitor"—our need and want to know how we're doing in relation to the goal—wanes. Additionally, not only do people find lofty goals difficult to monitor (and so they don't), but they also often struggle to believe such goals are actually attainable. Goals that are too large are often frustrating, because the gap between where we currently are and where we want to get is huge, and we have no idea how we'll close it (McGonigal, 2011). This feeling decreases motivation even to attempt the goal. Breaking a large, far-off goal down into small steps makes the goal feel more attainable, and if the goal feels attainable, monitoring progress (and adjusting accordingly) becomes more likely (Woolfolk et al., 2015). But as we will see in Chapter 5, working in small, discrete increments requires new learning for many of us.

Discomfort

The final dimension of purposeful practice is probably the most important: getting outside one's comfort zone. It is almost impossible to improve without going beyond what one already considers easy (Ericsson & Pool, 2016). For example, the principal who works at leading in-school professional development in the same way every time because it feels comfortable isn't going to get any better at it. As Ericsson and Pool (2016) state:

Getting out of your comfort zone means trying to do something that you couldn't do before. Sometimes you may find it relatively easy to accomplish that new thing, and then you keep pushing on. But sometimes you run into something that stops you cold and it seems like you'll never be able to do it. Finding ways around these barriers is one of the hidden keys to purposeful practice. (p. 19)

Generally, getting around these barriers is not about trying harder but about trying *differently,* coming at something from a different angle. Working with a teacher or a coach or a critical friend colleague who is already familiar with the different barriers one is likely to find and knows of potential strategies for overcoming them is a powerful strategy for learning to work differently. As we have said elsewhere, learning is about an opportunity to be challenged by things that are not consistent with our current ways of thinking and acting (see Katz & Dack, 2013). Intentionally engaging others who bring alternative perspectives is one important way of achieving this.

In summary, purposeful practice is about (a) having well-defined, specific goals; (b) engaging in focused practice sessions; (c) soliciting effective feedback; and (d) getting outside one's comfort zone. Like many of the most worthwhile things in life, purposeful practice is effortful and not easy. Deliberately feeling uncomfortable isn't something that most of us like or choose to do, and in fact we tend to avoid it (for an extensive treatment of this basic facet of human nature, see Katz & Dack, 2013). A salient and relevant finding from the expertise literature is that expert musicians who have engaged in enormous numbers of hours of purposeful practice over their lifetimes say that they find improvement difficult and not much fun (Ericsson et al., 1993). This is an important message about practice. It isn't that experts love to practice and do it for enjoyment; they do it because they understand that practice is essential to improvement (Ericsson & Pool, 2016). We see this as a key component of the leader-learning inquiry process discussed in Chapter 5.

THE PSYCHOLOGICAL FOUNDATIONS OF
COLLABORATIVE LEADER LEARNING

Remember that our goal in this chapter is to articulate the psychological underpinnings of the inquiry-driven Leader Learning Team structure and process described in detail in the next two chapters. So far, we've outlined what it means to get better through purposeful practice as a way of thinking about instructional leadership capacity building using an inquiry process. Now, we turn to a consideration of the "team" or collaborative aspect of this model of leader learning.

Earlier in this chapter we defined developing expertise as being about building richer schemas or mental representations. Essentially, developing expertise is about a quest for deep understanding. Having a deep understanding in a particular area, as we explained, allows for more precision but also more flexibility in responding to challenges, resulting in more effective solutions. From what we've said so far, it might seem like this quest for deep understanding is an individual pursuit. But importantly, our notion of the LLT relies on a collaborative setting in an evidence-informed way. As Supovitz (2006) writes, "The power of the idea of a professional learning community is that members of the group . . . engage together in challenges of practice so that their *understanding of those challenges grows deeper* [emphasis added] and is more unified" (p. 178). We know from the research that there is a social aspect to building deep understanding and that a collaborative setting, when implemented correctly, adds value to the work of an individual in terms of building deep understanding. Correct implementation—or the "right" kind of collaboration— is our focus in the remainder of this chapter.

In virtually all professional arenas, collaboration is considered to be a key mechanism for both learning and getting things done. Regardless of the specific collaborative structure (large group, small group, formal, informal), the inherent belief is that together is better than alone. Most people believe that once a collaborative team has been formed, good things will happen. However, that's often not the case. It's not just involving others, but rather what the group actually does that has the potential to make a difference. While "together is better" might be a popular belief, research tells us that it's an oversimplification; there are times when together might actually be worse than alone (Katz, 2010).

Why is it the case that some collaborative groups are productive while others are not? What is it that effective collaborative groups do, and how is that different from their less effective—or even detrimental—counterparts? Judith Warren Little (1990) offers a useful fourfold taxonomy for examining collaboration: storytelling and scanning for ideas, aid and assistance, sharing, and joint work. "Storytelling and scanning for ideas" refers to quick, informal exchanges between individuals that typically happen at a distance from the classroom. In "aid and assistance," mutual aid or help is readily available when it's asked for, but colleagues are unlikely to offer one another assistance in an unsolicited way. In "sharing," colleagues make aspects of their work available to others, but there is no commentary on the work and no dimension of challenge. It is in "joint work" where colleagues share responsibility and really believe that they need each other's contributions to succeed. In joint work, ideas are put on the table for discussion, analysis, debate, and challenge. People practicing joint work challenge one another's assumptions about teaching and learning, provide feedback to one another (and are also receptive to receiving it from others), and talk openly about differing views and opinions.

It is this notion of joint work that represents the value-added potential of collaboration, but in reality joint work is difficult and elusive. This is because there are a number of default practices that come with working together that act as barriers to learning; these practices have to be interrupted in an intentional way.

The Default Practices of Collaboration

As mentioned above, Little's (1990) notion of joint work—which includes analysis, debate, and challenge—is what lies at the heart of impactful collaboration. It is these aspects of "working together" that have the potential to push us toward the requisite deeper understanding for improvement. Recall that in Chapter 1 we reiterated that learning is about making permanent changes to previous ways of thinking and acting. Learning is about taking what we already know and do, having those ideas challenged, and making permanent changes where appropriate to think and act differently moving forward (Katz & Dack, 2013). Analysis, debate, and challenge facilitate this change process by showing us where our current ways of thinking and acting are in need of modification.

The difficulty, however, is that human beings work very hard to hold on to our current ways of thinking and acting, and to avoid the critical challenges that lead to real new learning (Katz & Dack, 2013). Although the goal of collaborative encounters is for the necessary components of joint work to be present, in reality they are often absent. We refer to collaborative encounters that are void of the key elements of joint work as "great discussions" (always in quotation marks because it's tongue-in-cheek!). When groups of people get together with the goal of learning or accomplishing something, there tends to be a significant amount of discussion. And people often leave these meetings and comment to themselves or to others that it was a "great discussion." But ultimately, there is no real evidence of sustainable change or learning.

Consider the notion of groupthink—that is, the stifling of individuality that occurs in a collective context. The idea behind groupthink is that if you put a group of people together and allow for a free-flowing discussion, the group tends to settle on a position for which there is already high agreement among members. This does wonders for preserving the status quo of thinking and practice, but nothing to change or advance it. Group members tend to fail to express different viewpoints because of a fear of conflict, and this often leads to poor decision making.

The term *groupthink* was coined by Irving Janis (1972), who focused primarily on poor political and military decisions that were a result of groupthink behaviors. For example, there is evidence that a number of historically poor decisions (such as the decision to launch the Bay of Pigs invasion of Cuba in 1960, the decision to cover up the Watergate break-in in 1972, and the decisions to launch the *Challenger* space shuttle in 1986 and the *Columbia* space shuttle in 2003) were influenced by groupthink (Lunenburg, 2010). Research has focused not only on the extreme circumstances in which groupthink has led to tragedy but also on the potential effects of groupthink within any collective setting. Essentially, being in a group, regardless of the context, can lead to a lack of variability in perspectives (Katz et al., 2009). Relatedly, the research on group brainstorming (as compared to individual brainstorming) shows that this exercise often suppresses creativity, a perfect example of how together can be worse than alone (Kohn & Smith, 2011). The culprit, once again, is the pressure for conformity in the collective context. "Great discussions" often involve a significant amount of *talking,* but with a narrow range of perspectives and few differences in opinions being shared. And this is a problem because, as we've said before, real new learning relies on access to diversity of opinion (Katz & Dack, 2013). In fact, research on what's known as social physics has found that people who are consistently creative and insightful spend a significant amount of time seeking out people with views and ideas that are different from their own (Pentland, 2015).

Diffusion of responsibility is another common consequence of typical collaborative work. Diffusion of responsibility refers to the idea that when people are in a group setting they are less likely to take personal responsibility than they would be if they were alone. Those with a background in social psychology will recall that research on this phenomenon began after the tragic death of Catherine (Kitty) Genovese in 1964. Genovese was murdered in a late-night attack in New York City, as she was on her way home from work. In the weeks following her murder, it was revealed that thirty-eight individuals had witnessed the attack, which took place over a period of more than thirty minutes, but not a single person responded in a way that might have saved her. While the original interpretation of the case was that no one cared enough to call for help, psychologists Bibb Latané and John Darley became interested in the story and began a line of investigative research (see Cialdini, 2007). Their seminal research, conducted in 1968, revealed that when a single individual witnessed an emergency, that person helped the victim 85 percent of the time (suggesting that people do in fact care about helping others), but when five bystanders were present, the victim received help only 31 percent of the time. The interpretation is that when multiple people are present, all of them take less responsibility than they would if they were on their own.

The idea of diffusion of responsibility—that we all do less in a group context than we would on our own—is also sometimes referred to as "social loafing." And it is familiar to most people in everyday contexts. We can all probably remember a time when we worked in a group and did far more than we should have because someone else appeared to be "slacking off." And many of us probably also remember a time when we worked in a group and relied a bit too much on others instead of pulling our own weight (i.e., when we were the social loafer!). It's often the case that in "great discussions" no one engages in the hard work of learning because everyone believes that someone else will ultimately own the agenda and move it forward (Katz et al., 2009).

In addition to groupthink and diffusion of responsibility, there are further reasons why the core components of joint work—such as analysis, debate, and challenge—are often absent from collaborative learning, and why it is difficult for "great discussions" to ultimately translate into real and sustained changes. As we have mentioned, human beings tend to shy away from change more than they embrace it. Joint work is really about changing our ways of thinking and acting, but in reality most of us (because we're human) don't want to change! While we all know that change is difficult, many of us believe that we are more open to change than we truly are. In reality, many people operate in a learning environment in a way that protects their current beliefs and practices.

Take the confirmation bias, for example—that is, the idea that once people have a hypothesis about something, they tend to look only for things that confirm it and disregard those that challenge it. The confirmation bias, well supported by research, essentially shows that people tend to engage with the world in a way that confirms what they already think, believe, know, and do, and that they work hard to avoid evidence to the contrary. In *Intentional Interruption*, we describe the way people tend to approach a professional reading activity, as an example, by highlighting parts of the reading that say things they already believe and ignoring the parts that don't! And so, in "great discussions" it is often the case that people are paying significant attention to the ideas they hear that confirm their existing beliefs and practices while ignoring those that don't (which is problematic for learning because real learning is about *changing* beliefs and practices) (Katz & Dack, 2013).

An additional aspect of human nature that can hinder joint work is the "culture of niceness" (Elmore, 2007). In the culture of niceness, people are so worried about hurting one another's feelings that beliefs, ideas, and practices get superficially validated in collaborative exchanges. People often avoid professional conflict or challenge in order to protect the feelings of others, but as a result they give up the opportunities for critical challenge that can lead to deep understanding and changed practice. While educators might be particularly prone to this culture of niceness, it has certainly been described in other arenas as well. A CEO that we know well once said, "The biggest problem facing my organization is that we all tiptoe around each other, afraid of hurting one another's feelings if we say what we're really thinking. And so we just smile at each other and say 'great idea' and then talk behind one another's backs." From our perspective, the issue isn't so much about wanting to be nice, but rather about needing to be superficial in order to be nice. We regularly see "great discussions" characterized by a superficial niceness (which we have come to call "superfice") that makes people feel good but does not provide the critical challenge that is necessary to lead to real new learning.

In addition to these default practices of collaborative behavior that impede the likelihood of joint work, we have to worry about the issue of quality control in "great discussions" (Katz et al., 2009). It is certainly the intent for groups of people working together to spread ideas and practices, but what happens when the ideas and practices being spread are not good ones? We've often said that the only thing worse than a bad idea is a bad idea in a lot of places! There is evidence in the literature for this lack of quality control in collaborative settings. In his book *Influence* (2007), which looks at the psychology of persuasion, Robert Cialdini describes the phenomenon of people imitating one another without thinking critically (or even at all) about what they're doing. He provides compelling examples of the way people use social evidence to make decisions, particularly in situations where they are uncertain about what is correct. Television shows use canned laughter to get audiences to laugh ("It must be funny if others are laughing!"), bartenders put some of their own money in their tip jars at the beginning of the night ("Look how many people have tipped; I should do it too!"), and advertisers tell us how well products are selling ("So many people are buying this product, it must be something I need!"). The fact that people determine the way to think and act based on their perceptions of how others are thinking and acting is dangerous, and we have seen it happen time and time again in collaborative settings that fail to interrogate how "good" the ideas and practices are that are being shared.

It's evident that there are some fairly powerful default practices at work in collaborative settings, many of which get in the way of joint work. Yet joint work is necessary for collaborative exchanges to be effective. Returning to Supovitz's (2006) finding that impactful professional learning communities involve "members of the group . . . [engaging] together in challenges of practice so that their understanding of those challenges grows deeper and is more unified" (p. 178), we would do well to ask how such learning communities get beyond the default practices of "great discussions." How is it that some collaborative groups are different? We consider this next.

From "Great Discussions" to Focused Learning Conversations: The Value of Protocols

Pixar, the computer animation film studio that we all know, has produced seventeen feature films, and all have been box-office successes. When you have that kind of repeated success it's because of more than just luck; intentional and deliberate forces must be at work. Ed Catmull (2014), president of Pixar, has explained why the company does so well:

> Our decision making is better when we draw on the collective knowledge and unvarnished opinions of the group. Candor is the key to collaborating effectively. Lack of candor leads to dysfunctional environments. So how can a manager ensure that his or her working group, department, or company embraces candor? By putting mechanisms in place that explicitly say it is valuable. (p. 1)

Pixar recognizes that candor is crucial to effective collaboration—and subsequent success—because it's candor that provides the critical challenge necessary to drive improvement. But importantly, Pixar also recognizes that candor won't just appear spontaneously within collaborative settings. Catmull (2014) explicitly refers to the fear of hurting someone's feelings as an obstacle to candor. And he also notes that one of the biggest challenges of candor is that the person receiving the feedback isn't always in a position to want to hear it.

In our language, Pixar has figured out how to move beyond "great discussions" by "putting mechanisms in place" that explicitly say that candor is valuable and, in fact, necessary.

We've been exploring such mechanisms in our own work, and we've found that the key tenets of joint work are much more likely to occur in a focused "learning conversation" than in a free-flowing "great discussion." A learning conversation is a planned and systematic approach to professional dialogue that supports teachers/leaders to reflect on their practice. As a result, the teacher/leader gains new knowledge and uses it to improve his or her practice (General Teaching Council of England, 2004). The essential ingredients of focused learning conversations that make them qualitatively different from "great discussions" is that they are both *planned* and *systematic*. Focused learning conversations do not just happen on their own when groups of people get together to "discuss"; rather, they are a result of intentional, systematic planning of the learning opportunity.

Successful collaborative groups often use protocols to structure their learning conversations in planned and systematic ways. Protocols are structured sets of guidelines designed to promote effective and efficient communication and problem solving. They help the group focus on the task at hand and mitigate the default practices of collaboration described above. Protocols can also ensure that conversations are shared equally among group members, rather than dominated by a few people, which is an important factor in how well a group performs (Pentland, 2015).

There are many different kinds of protocols, and entire books have been written to describe all the different choices and the particular scenarios in which they work best (e.g., see Easton, 2009; McDonald, Mohr, Dichter, & McDonald, 2007). For example, there are protocols to explore a problem of practice, assess whether an assignment meets a teacher's goals, look at student work samples, help teachers determine what and how students are thinking, and provide feedback on a teacher's assignment, among many others. Protocols don't need to be fancy or overly complicated in their instructions; what they need to do is provide a structure that forces people to do things they wouldn't naturally do. Essentially, protocols for collaborative groups work by intentionally interrupting the default practices of collaboration found in "great discussions" and, in doing so, bring the groups closer to joint work.

Think about how a protocol might intentionally interrupt the culture of niceness, for example. When providing feedback to one another in typical "great discussions," people tend to avoid any kind of comment that could be interpreted as critical of someone else's practice. This is due to a belief that such feedback isn't "nice" because it takes issue with the person's value and worth as a professional. Alternatively, when there is some kind of constructive feedback to provide, it often gets coupled with a superficially positive comment to maintain the facade of "niceness." Protocols can help to interrupt this propensity to avoid challenge by providing step-by-step instructions for how to talk about someone else's practice and provide feedback on it in a way that separates person from practice, so that people take less personal offense when their practices are challenged.

In much the same way, protocols can intentionally interrupt groupthink, diffusion of responsibility, and the confirmation bias. A protocol can interrupt the notion of groupthink by instructing individuals to come up with a wide and varied range of ideas instead of prematurely reaching consensus. A protocol can interrupt diffusion of responsibility by assigning specific roles to particular individuals, which has been shown to increase responsiveness and accountability (see, e.g., Cialdini, 2007). And a protocol can interrupt people's propensity to fall prey to the confirmation bias by forcing them to attend to perspectives that are contrary to their own. In Chapter 6, we provide a detailed description of our Learning Conversations Protocol, which we have designed to use with Leader Learning Teams to intentionally interrupt "great discussions" and enable true professional learning.

Recall that our intention in this chapter has been to provide the research foundation for the LLT model that we describe and illustrate in the remaining chapters of this book.

We have developed the LLT process and all of its supporting tools in keeping with this research base, and as we've noted several times now, successful implementation and utilization of the model require an understanding of the "why" behind it.

TIME FOR REFLECTION

1. Which elements of purposeful practice have you experienced in your own professional life? What might it look like to bring the essential elements of purposeful practice into your school's professional learning space?

2. Since developing expertise is defined as building rich schemas through deep understanding, which collective schemas are you in the process of changing in your school, and how are you doing this?

3. How have you experienced groupthink in your school, and what impact did this thinking have on your school?

5

Getting Better at "Influence" Through Leader Learning Inquiries

Earlier in this book we made reference to our example principal's participation in a learning team with some of his school administrator colleagues, noting that this was a key part of his learning how to "influence" others through intelligent, responsive leadership practice. Remember, intelligent, responsive schools require intelligent, responsive leadership. And, as we've argued, intelligent, responsive leadership is a capacity that can be developed through purposeful practice. This is what it means to get better as a leader. Our Leader Learning Team (LLT) process is the "how" of purposeful practice for leaders. It's the way leaders learn to develop intelligent, responsive practice. Chapter 4 provided the backdrop for this process, which we describe in this chapter and the next. Taken together, these two chapters unpack the LLT model, which functions as an inquiry-based vehicle for building leadership capacity. Specifically, in this chapter we describe how adaptive challenges around the notion of "leadership as influence" are transformed into investigable leadership inquiry questions that take a capacity-building orientation. In Chapter 6, we demonstrate how groups of administrators engage in highly structured "critical friend" interactions to enable true professional learning in themselves and others. Across the two chapters we also describe the processes and resources that we use to guide the successful implementation of LLTs. Throughout both chapters, we refer back to the research base cited in Chapter 4.

WHAT ARE LEADER LEARNING TEAMS?

Leader Learning Teams are vehicles for building instructional leadership capacity through leadership learning inquiries. An LLT involves a small group (usually five or six people) of school or district leaders who work together as "critical friends." Each leader is individually working to tackle his or her own leadership inquiry that has emerged as a challenge of professional practice, with members of the group acting as critical friends to support one another's inquiries. To an outsider, LLTs might look like small groups of leaders who meet every six weeks or so to "talk" about professional issues of mutual interest. Someone intimately connected to the process, however, knows that what happens at an LLT meeting is much more than a "great discussion." Rather, it is a structured conversation that serves as a critical analysis of an individual's work that is intended to push all group members' thinking and learning beyond what they could accomplish on their own. Someone intimately connected to the process also knows that much of the work of the LLT is actually happening between meetings, when each leader is thoughtfully planning learning moves as part of his or her inquiry, enacting these moves, and reflecting on what has been learned and where the learning should go next. These ideas are explicated throughout this chapter and the next.

Although this book illustrates the LLT structure and process mainly from the perspective of *school* leaders, it is important to note that other leader groups have also adapted it for their own contexts. We work with many groups of district leaders who use this same process of inquiry and collaborative analysis, and other leader groups (such as teacher leaders) use it as well. Whether it's a group of school leaders looking to improve their instructional leadership practice as they support their "classes" of teachers (Timperley, 2011) or a group of district leaders looking to get better as they support their "classes" of school leaders, the process is the same.

LEADERSHIP LEARNING INQUIRIES

In Chapter 4, we described what it means to do intentional work to "get better." We discussed the research that has shown that without intentional efforts toward improvement, abilities tend to stagnate or even decline over time, and we emphasized instructional leadership as a place where leaders cannot allow that to happen. Leadership inquiries are the vehicle for learning how to get better at particular aspects of instructional leadership. In Leader Learning Teams, each leader participant works through an inquiry process to investigate and learn about his or her own leadership challenge of practice.

In school systems, everyone has a "class" (Timperley, 2011). Teachers have classes of students, school leaders have classes of teachers, and district leaders have classes of school leaders. The challenges of practice that leaders (school or district) experience emerge from where they are feeling stuck in relation to being able to influence their classes with respect to a school improvement agenda. In the case of school leaders, this relates to where a principal is stuck with respect to influencing teachers (all or some) to engage in the kind of professional learning that has an impact on teaching practice around an area of focus as determined by data. In the case of district leaders, this relates to where a leader is stuck with respect to influencing school leaders as they develop instructional leadership capacity.

A leadership challenge of practice is an adaptive challenge (Heifetz, Grashow, & Linsky, 2009); no algorithm exists that specifies how to solve the problem, and so learning through inquiry is required. Working through the challenge of practice using an inquiry process creates a space for the leader to get better at the relevant aspects of instructional leadership in a way that is just in time, job embedded, and needs based. And we know that just in time, job embedded, and needs based are the essential ingredients in the most impactful professional learning (Katz & Dack, 2013).

As we described in Chapter 4, recent research has shown that leaders who believe their major role is to evaluate their own impact are among the most effective (see Hattie, 2015). Leadership inquiries are centered on the idea of leaders evaluating their impact on others as they work to answer two key questions: Am I getting better? and How do I know? A leadership inquiry is a space where a leader is committed to learning how to get better at "influencing" his or her "class."

For school leaders, leadership challenges of practice grow out of the plan for school improvement that the leader—ideally in collaboration with a team of teachers—has developed. The school improvement plan articulates what students need to learn (based on evidence) and what teachers need to learn to support what students need to learn (also based on evidence). The leader then articulates where he or she is feeling stuck with respect to supporting his or her class of teachers to engage in the necessary professional learning and develops an inquiry question to support his or her own learning about influence in this context.

Consider this example from a principal we know well, the leader of a midsize elementary school. The school's improvement focus for students was on changing student mindset with respect to mathematical abilities. This focus arose from school data showing that students were struggling with mathematics, as compared to reading and writing, on large-scale assessments, as well as on other forms of assessment. Importantly, when surveyed, only 20 percent of students in the school reported that they believed they were able to change their mathematical skills (that is, they had a fairly fixed mindset with respect to math; they believed their math abilities to be unchangeable). In a teacher survey, the principal found that about half of the teachers had a strong understanding of the concept of growth mindset (the idea that intelligence can be developed), but only 10 percent reported that they knew what kinds of strategies to use to try to encourage a growth mindset for students in math. The principal also found that 75 percent of the teachers had a fixed mindset about their own mathematical abilities. Given the research showing the positive impact of growth mindset on motivation, effort, and achievement in math (e.g., Blackwell, Trzesniewski, & Dweck, 2007; Good, Aronson, & Inzlicht, 2003), the principal, with support of the school improvement team, decided that the teacher improvement focus in the school needed to be on learning effective strategies for changing student mindset in math. The theory of action was that if teachers learned how to encourage a growth mindset in students, then they would engage in teaching strategies to support students to develop a growth mindset in math. And if students had more of a growth mindset in math, they would engage in behaviors that would ultimately improve their mathematical understanding and achievement. This, then, was the school's focus for improvement.

When this principal was asked where she was feeling stuck in relation to implementing this improvement plan, she stated that it was not with respect to understanding the notion of growth mindset as it relates to math. In fact, she was fairly confident that she had a strong grasp of the concept of mindset, and how it relates to math in particular. She believed that she was able to support teachers as they learned about growth mindset, and she was attempting to do so with teachers individually and in the school's professional learning community (PLC). Where this principal was feeling stuck was with respect to getting teachers to buy into the work of the PLC and to believe that the work was as important as she believed it was. As she once said to us, "Where I am stuck is that I feel like I alone own the PLC work. I don't know that there is a sense of urgency for many members of this group, and I wonder: What would happen if I walked away from the PLC? Who would own the learning? Would it happen at all without me?" The principal's concern was that if teachers were not truly engaged in the work of the PLC, there would be no opportunity for real professional learning to take place. And without real professional learning, there would be no change in classroom practice or, ultimately, in student achievement.

This principal was facing an adaptive challenge, in that the knowledge about how to move forward needed to be developed. Many of us can sympathize with this principal's challenge of wanting (and needing) to influence others to take ownership over professional learning, but most of us have no idea what to do about it. There is no algorithm for this, which is what makes the challenge adaptive in nature. In fact, this adaptive challenge emerged out of various "intelligent expectations" being implemented in the district and the school. Through informed prescription, the school had a detailed process for determining an evidence-based, authentic school improvement focus (which this school determined to be a growth mindset in math). The school was also using the prescribed PLC structure as a vehicle for taking up this improvement need. And in the effort to implement these prescriptions, an adaptive challenge—how to get people to take ownership over their learning in the PLC—emerged. Taking up this leadership challenge of practice shifted this principal's stance to a responsive one—she had to figure it out. She defined her personal inquiry question as "How do I learn how to lead people who don't feel personally connected to the PLC and get them to take ownership over the learning?" This principal understood that her role, as instructional leader, was to exercise influence to ensure that her "class" was engaging in the kind of professional learning that would improve teaching practice (and subsequently student learning). But she didn't know how to do it! She knew that she wouldn't get better at influencing teachers without intentional new learning for herself, and it would need to be learning that took the form of purposeful practice.

This principal was working as part of a Leader Learning Team with five other school leaders. Each principal was working on his or her own individual inquiry that responded to a personal leadership challenge of practice like the one just described. And while the contents and contexts of these inquiries were different, what united them was that they were all about getting better at influence. While each leader was engaging in his or her own inquiry, the function of the group was to process each individual's work collaboratively, adding value to all inquiries by thinking them through together. We describe the collaborative aspect of the LLT in the following chapter. In the rest of this chapter, we detail our process for scaffolding leaders to define and refine their inquiry questions (the area in which they need to get better) and for guiding them through the inquiry work itself (using the ideas of purposeful practice).

Developing a Leadership Inquiry Question Using Our Leadership Inquiry Template

Over the past few years we have developed and refined the following set of questions, which we use to scaffold leaders to determine an authentic, needs-based challenge of practice. The questions are explained in detail below.

What are your school improvement priorities?

- Student learning foci:
  - Evidence (that this needs to be an area of focus for students):
- Teacher learning foci:
  - Evidence (that this needs to be an area of focus for teachers):

Where are you stuck as a leader in this school improvement process? On what, and with whom?

What leader learning opportunity does this define for you? (Your adaptive challenge defines your leadership inquiry question.)

- Inquiry question: How do I learn how to . . . ?

What's the transfer potential from your learning, in terms of intelligent leadership practices?

First, the leader is asked to articulate what his or her school improvement priorities are, citing the evidence that has been used in developing the school's improvement plan. Specifically, the leader is asked to identify the student learning foci along with the supporting evidence of need. The leader is then asked to identify the teacher learning foci, again with supporting evidence of need. The principal in our example above answered these first questions as follows.

What are your school improvement priorities?

- **Student learning focus:** Mindset in math—students need to believe that they can grow their mathematical abilities.
  - **Evidence (that this needs to be an area of focus for students):**
    1. 4-year EQAO [large-scale centralized assessment] math data fluctuate, with no clear improvement trend (67%, 81%, 64%, and 78%) of students at or above the standard over the past 4 years.
    2. 2013–14 EQAO student questionnaire data reveal that 37% of students check their work for mistakes and 47% are able to answer difficult math questions.
    3. 18% of students who met the standard in mathematics in Grade 3 do not meet the standard in Grade 6 (compared to 2% in reading and 4% in writing).
    4. And most important, 1 in 5 students asked in this school believe that they have the ability to change their mathematical skills (survey data).
- **Teacher learning focus:** Teachers need to learn effective strategies for changing student mindset.
  - **Evidence (that this needs to be an area of focus for teachers):**
    1. All teachers in the school have heard about a growth mindset, but only 50% really understand it (based on survey responses).
    2. Only 10% of teachers reported that they think they know effective strategies for changing student mindset in math.
    3. 75% of teachers have a fixed mindset about their own math skills.

The questions about student and teacher learning needs are included on our template to ensure that the inquiry question that the leader identifies (the place where he or she is committed to learning how to get better) is truly grounded in the school's improvement needs. This is essential because a positive impact on student success is intended to always be at the heart of this work. In Chapter 1 we explicated our theory of action for school improvement, which drives the work of a leadership inquiry. If, as we explained, a student learning need drives a teacher learning need, and a teacher learning need drives a leader learning need, then determining a leader learning need must be traceable back to students. In fact, we have found that when a leader struggles to articulate a student learning need in academic or social/emotional terms, this makes it very difficult to articulate (and thus respond to) an authentic teacher learning need. In turn, it becomes virtually impossible to undertake an authentic leadership inquiry that is about influence and is just in time, job embedded, and needs based.

Our next question asks the school leader to identify where he or she is feeling stuck in terms of influencing the school improvement process. Essentially, where does the leader feel that he or she is "hitting a wall" and not able to proceed when it comes to moving the school improvement process forward, specifically in relation to influencing his or her "class" of teachers? This is where the idea of an adaptive challenge emerges, in that it is intended to be something that the leader does not know how to do. The principal in our example answered the next question in the following way:

Where are you stuck as a leader in this school improvement process? On what, and with whom?

I have done a lot of professional learning around growth mindset, and even about growth mindset in math in particular, and I believe that I am able to support teachers as they learn about this. I have been doing this all year in the PLC and one-on-one, and we seem to be moving forward slowly. Where I am stuck is that I feel like I alone own the PLC work. I don't know that there is a sense of urgency for many members of this group, or that they really feel they need to learn this, and I wonder: What would happen if I walked away from the PLC? Who would own the learning? Would it happen at all without me?

I don't feel this (lack of ownership of professional learning) is an issue with every single teacher, but it is with many of them (probably three-quarters).

The leader is then asked to use this "stuck space" to define an inquiry-based professional learning opportunity. In the case of this principal, she defined the following inquiry question:

> **What leader learning opportunity does this define for you? (Your adaptive challenge defines your leadership inquiry question.)**
>
> - **Inquiry question:** How do I learn how to . . . ?
>
> How do I learn how to lead people who might not feel personally connected to the PLC and get them to take ownership over the learning?

Importantly, by using the question stem of "How do I learn how to . . . ," the template encourages leaders to approach their inquiry in terms of what they are looking to *learn* rather than what they are looking to *do*. This focus on learning, rather than on doing, is carried throughout the inquiry process as each move that the leader undertakes in the inquiry (as described below) has learning, rather than activity, as the objective.

The "What" of a Leadership Inquiry

Our work with school leaders across numerous districts has exposed us to a wealth of inquiry questions that grow out of leaders' challenges of professional practice. One important distinction that leaders must make in determining a focus for a leadership inquiry is between their focus for school improvement and the stuck space that has emerged from this school improvement focus. In the case of the principal in our example, while her challenge of practice *emerges* from her school improvement focus on mindset in math, the school improvement focus is not her inquiry question. She is not asking, "How do I lead school improvement?" Instead, she is focusing on one particular implementation-related area where she is struggling to have influence—in this case, getting other people to own the work of the PLC. This distinction is important because a leadership inquiry cannot cover the entire school improvement focus, since opportunities to privilege depth (as in a *deep* understanding) over breadth would be impossible. As we state in *Intentional Interruption*:

> A learning focus, by definition, is narrow. It needs to be narrow enough so as to allow teachers [or leaders] to engage in a professional learning process that works to enhance depth of understanding. Breadth and depth are a trade off. A mile wide means an inch deep, and we know that [an inch deep] doesn't work when it comes to changing practice. But a mile deep means an inch wide. And that means we have to be sure that we've got the right inch! (Katz & Dack, 2013, p. 39)

Because a leadership inquiry needs to have a narrow focus, the questions on our template help to ensure that the focus is the "right" one (i.e., needs based, rather than "pick a topic").

Casual observers might look at a narrow leadership inquiry question and wonder whether it's enough. Consider the principal in our example. Someone might look at her inquiry and say, "How can you focus only on learning how to get teachers committed to the PLC when you have an entire school to run?" We respond to this question the same way we respond when people are worried about a teacher learning focus being too narrow. As we continue in *Intentional Interruption*:

> When we first started to work with the notion of focus in various schools and districts, an important and problematic unintended consequence emerged that we subsequently identified and unpacked in our research (Katz & Dack, 2009). Practitioners engaged with the concept of focus through the dominant culture of activity, rather than an alternative culture of learning. What this meant was that focus was interpreted as a teaching focus, not a learning focus. Teachers constantly asked us how they could possibly prioritize something as narrow as "inferring in reading for meaning" in their teaching, given the breadth of the required formal curriculum.

A critical distinction was missing. A focus on inferring means that teachers are committed to privileging their own professional *learning* about inferring. However, they are still *teaching* the entire curriculum. Identifying a focus doesn't mean that you don't care about other things. It's simply about moving an urgent (professional) learning need to the foreground. (p. 39)

We make the same argument here. Your learning needs and your job aren't synonymous. As a school or district leader you have a whole job to do that is outside your leadership inquiry, and you likely already know how to do most of it. We are not suggesting that an inquiry narrows that job. The distinction is that you have identified a narrow slice for the purpose of *learning.* You are *doing* your entire job, yet learning about one narrow piece at a time. You go an inch wide—but a mile deep—in learning about one thing, and then once you have evidence to suggest that you no longer have that learning need, you move on to the next inch.

Another important distinction when it comes to defining a leadership inquiry question is between something a leader must learn how to do and something the leader simply needs to do. As we mentioned in Chapter 4, for example, our work with school and district leaders has shown us that *monitoring* is commonly defined as a challenge of professional practice. At the school leader level, principals often find it challenging to monitor the school's improvement focus in relation to teacher practice. At the district level, leaders often find it challenging to monitor a school's improvement focus in relation to school leader practice. Importantly, when leaders define an inquiry question in relation to monitoring, they must think about whether they need to learn how to monitor or whether they know how to monitor but simply need to do it. If the latter is the case, it doesn't make for a good inquiry question because it's not really about learning.

This emphasizes how personal a leadership inquiry question really is. One leader might truly not know what it means to monitor a school's improvement focus, while another might *know* how to do it but need to push him- or herself to *actually* do it. A Leader Learning Team is always made up of leaders with different levels of experience and capacity, so the inquiry questions defined will be different. One school leader, for example, might be feeling stuck around learning how to get teachers to care about the PLC work (as in our example above), while another might be stuck on learning how to lead a PLC itself. It is important to recognize and encourage the variability within an LLT and to understand that each leader needs to inquire around a challenge of professional practice that is authentic and urgent for him- or herself, not for others. As we said earlier, the common denominator that will unite all LLT members, regardless of content or context, is that they will all be learning about leadership as influence.

Consider the following example, from a different school principal.

What are your school improvement priorities?

- **Student learning focus:** Students need to get better at improving their written work after receiving teacher feedback.

    - **Evidence (that this needs to be an area of focus for students):** Data (both anecdotal and assessment based) show that students' written work after receiving teacher feedback is only marginally better in terms of meeting teacher expectations than it was on the first round.

- **Teacher learning focus:** Descriptive feedback.

    - **Evidence (that this needs to be an area of focus for teachers):** The evidence that I have gathered and looked at (graded student work samples) shows that teachers are not using descriptive feedback in assessing written student work.

Where are you stuck as a leader in this school improvement process? On what, and with whom?

Where I am stuck is that I have two teachers, call them A and B, who sit in our staff meetings and PLC meetings (where we intentionally try to work on the above) and constantly whisper to each other, roll their eyes, and show negative body language such as crossed arms. I worry about this because these teachers have a long history at this school, are well liked by staff, are fairly influential with other teachers, and are close friends. One is stronger than the other in terms of teaching practice, but neither is where I would like them to be. I worry that their negativity is

---

(Continued)

(Continued)

going to impact others. I believe that if I knew how to get these two on board with our school improvement focus there would be the potential to positively impact other staff and help everyone move forward.

What leader learning opportunity does this define for you? (Your adaptive challenge defines your leadership inquiry question.)

- **Inquiry question:** How do I learn how to . . . ?

How do I learn how to move these two teachers forward in a positive way?

In this example, the inquiry question is again not specifically related to the school's improvement focus, which in this case is about using descriptive feedback to help students improve, but it originates with an implementation challenge there. It is a leader asking how she can learn what she needs to do to positively influence two seemingly negative but potentially influential teachers. Importantly, you will notice that she has not been specific in her inquiry question in terms of *what* she is looking to have an impact on. The question doesn't read, "How do I learn how to motivate these teachers?" or "How do I learn how to get these teachers to understand that they have something to learn in order to improve their practice?" or "How do I learn how to help these teachers be vulnerable and take an open-to-learning stance?" These questions all involve potential hypotheses about what might be behind the problematic behaviors exhibited by these teachers. Through the process of learning via the inquiry (which we describe below), the principal can investigate which, if any, of these hypotheses might be accurate, resulting in a subsequent inquiry question that is more refined. But for now, without knowing more about what's behind these behaviors, the principal has simply defined her inquiry question as "How do I learn how to move these two teachers forward in a positive way?"

Both of the examples presented above relate to a school leader's ability to better understand people in order to be influential. Let's consider one more example from a principal of a large secondary school, which is different in nature from the previous ones.

What are your school improvement priorities?

- **Student learning focus:** Self-regulation—both in learning environments and in behavior.

  ○ **Academic evidence:**

  Teachers have reported that:

  Students do not know how to manage their workload. Students need significant support in starting their work. Students do not check their work for mistakes.

  ○ **Behavior evidence:**

  Over the past 3 years the number of student altercations (with one another and with teachers) that have ended up in the office has increased by about 20%.

  Students cannot separate from their electronic devices.

- **Teacher learning focus:** We need to learn more about self-regulation (academic and behavior) to better support students in this skill.

  ○ **Evidence:** Just under half of our teachers really understand self-regulation (survey responses), and only one-quarter report that they use strategies to teach self-regulation to students.

Where are you stuck as a leader in this school improvement process? On what, and with whom?

Differentiation. It seems that I have 3 groups of teachers. Those who don't really understand self-regulation, those who know what it is about but don't regularly use strategies to teach it, and those that have strong understanding and practice. I want our school's professional learning agenda to meet everyone's needs, but I don't know how to effectively differentiate. And making things even more complicated, the teachers in the 3 groups are spread across different departments, yet much of our professional learning happens at the department level.

What leader learning opportunity does this define for you? (Your adaptive challenge defines your leadership inquiry question.)

- **Inquiry question:** How do I learn how to . . . ?

How do I learn how to differentiate professional learning for teachers so that it meets each teacher's learning needs?

This example has differentiation at the heart of the inquiry question. Although this leader's inquiry is not focused on learning how to understand people per se, as in the previous two examples, it is still centered on leadership as influence. In this case, the leader is working to learn how to ensure that she is able to influence each teacher at the school in moving forward with his or her own professional learning, which is a challenge when teachers are in such varied places both literally and figuratively.

The "Who" of a Leadership Inquiry

One notable way in which the examples above differ is that in the first example (learning how to influence teachers to take ownership over the PLC) and the third (learning how to differentiate professional learning), the inquiry question grows out of a challenge that the principal is experiencing with the "class" of teachers *in general* (perhaps not all of them, but at least most of them). In the second example, however, the principal clearly articulates that this is a challenge that she is experiencing with two teachers in particular. All three of these examples are challenges of practice that are worthy learning spaces for leaders, but for different reasons. The value of the inquiry might be more obvious in the first and third examples, given that the challenges involve most of the teachers in the principals' schools. You can clearly see how the principals would be getting "bang for their buck" by learning how to move forward in these contexts. In the second example, however, where the challenge involves only two teachers, one might ask whether it is a "good" inquiry question.

Aside from the obvious fact that two can influence many, it is important to ask whether these two teachers are *representative* of a broader class. We would say that an inquiry focused on learning how to influence only one or two teachers is worth a leader's valuable (and limited) learning time if the teachers are representative examples of a broader class of others that the principal might reasonably expect to encounter in the future—in other words, if the profile of the challenge is one likely to come up again with other people or in other places.

In this example, the answer to the question of representativeness is yes. Teachers A and B in the second example might be the only ones in that principal's school at the given moment with that particular behavioral profile, but the idea of teachers who do not believe that they have anything to learn, or are not motivated to engage in professional learning, or are afraid to show what they don't know, is not unique. Unfortunately, this is likely not the last time this principal is going to encounter something that looks like this! Learning how to move forward with these teachers in a positive way is certainly something that this principal will use again in her career, likely sooner rather than later.

In other cases, however, we have seen leaders define their inquiries around particular individuals who are unique, in which case the potential to transfer the learning to new situations becomes questionable. For example, one principal began an inquiry to learn how to influence a teacher in her school who was particularly resistant to change, and through her inquiry, discovered that this teacher was suffering from obsessive–compulsive disorder, which was having a serious impact on her classroom practice. While this situation continued to be a problem that the principal needed to manage in a most sensitive manner, she decided that it was no longer a good one to learn from, inquiry-wise, because the potential to transfer the learning to new contexts was low. As such, she shifted her inquiry to learning how to get better in relation to a different challenge of practice that was urgent and needs based for her.

Defining a Learning Case, If Necessary

Inquiries that are focused on one or two individuals work to support transferable learning about influence as long as the "representative" criterion is kept in mind. In fact, it is often easier to plan and monitor small learning moves (as described below) when working with a small number of individuals rather than with the "class" as a whole. Because of this, when leadership inquiries are focused on learning how to influence a large number of individuals (as in the first and third examples above), we often encourage the leader to select a "learning case" to work with. As we know from the research on purposeful practice, a leadership inquiry is a lot of work. Each "learning move," as you will see, needs to be carefully planned, enacted, assessed, and reflected upon. While some learning moves might involve a number of people at once (e.g., if a principal tries a move at a staff meeting), others might target individuals one-on-one (e.g., through one-on-one conversations with staff members). It wouldn't be sensible to try a move like one-on-one conversation with multiple people before knowing if it works with one or two, because it's time-consuming and could potentially have an unintended negative impact. Therefore, we encourage leaders to select a subset of their class to focus on for learning. A school leader might learn by focusing on one or two teachers who are representative of the broader class of teachers more generally, or perhaps a small number of teachers who already constitute a natural grouping (e.g., teachers in one particular department). We refer to this focused subset as a leader's learning case.

The Importance of Transferability

The final question on the front end of our leadership inquiry template—which we have not yet addressed—asks the leader to hypothesize about the transfer potential of the learning from the inquiry. In essence, this is the bang-for-the-buck question, and it is crucial. The function of a leadership inquiry is for an individual to engage in purposeful practice in order to get better at some aspect of leadership. Using the scaffolding questions just described, the leader determines what he or she needs to learn about in order to move his or her class forward. The learning, as we have seen, is focused, sometimes on a small subset of the leader's class. Importantly, however, the learning is not meant to be confined to the specific context of the inquiry; rather, it is intended to be transferred to other analogous, high-frequency situations. Real new learning, as we've said before, is permanent, and the true litmus test for permanent learning is transferability (Katz & Dack, 2013).

We often refer to the particular context of a leadership inquiry as the "petri dish" for learning—the small, contained space in which knowledge can grow. The idea is that the petri dish provides an environment in which deep understanding is allowed to grow, so that it can ultimately be transferred out and applied elsewhere. The template asks leaders to hypothesize about transfer potential, about what they hope to add to their influence tool kits more generally so that the next time they're in a similar situation they won't be starting from scratch. In fact, the idea is for individuals to spend time going deep and engaging in responsive inquiry in order to build some intelligent expectations around leadership for future use. This is what we meant in Chapter 2 when we wrote that "today's responsive can be tomorrow's intelligent." We see the interplay between intelligent and responsive here, in that an inquiry that grows out of an adaptive challenge that requires a responsive stance can drive a leader to build some intelligent practices to depend and draw upon in the future.

All three of the principals described in the examples above can expect to face similar challenges of influence again. The first principal is going to encounter teachers who aren't taking ownership over their learning in the future, the second will be faced with more PLC eye rollers in the future, and the third will need to deal with teachers in different places on the learning continuum in the future. As a concrete illustration, the principal in the first example answered that final question in this way:

What's the transfer potential from your learning, in terms of intelligent leadership practices?

This will help me learn about improving the instructional program (specifically providing instructional support and monitoring progress in student learning and school improvement). It will also help with developing the organization and building relationships and developing people.

THE "HOW" OF A LEADERSHIP INQUIRY

Thus far we have described the process for arriving at a leadership inquiry question that each leader in a Leader Learning Team will individually determine and investigate. The next logical question is, "So now what? How do I respond to my challenge of practice?" The answer is that you turn the inquiry question into a just-in-time, job-embedded, needs-based learning opportunity. You reframe the question, from "How do I do it?" to "How do I *learn* how to do it?" You privilege the learning and let the doing follow. As we often say, you do the work by learning the work! The sequence in this statement is important here, and it is reversed from what others might argue when they say if you just "do" you'll automatically learn. From our perspective, if you make the learning the intentional objective, the improved doing will follow. The research on purposeful practice supports this assertion.

In Chapter 4 we learned that you're not going to improve by just continuing to do. We learned that many hours of repetitive "doing" won't lead to improvement, and under those conditions, abilities might actually decline. Purposeful practice is about going outside one's comfort zone; using focused, goal-driven activity to improve an area of weakness; and making changes based on feedback received. You will see how these ideas all appear in the inquiry process we describe below.

In *Intentional Interruption* (Katz & Dack, 2013), we discuss the notion of inquiry as the discipline of working through a framework like the one shown here (Hakkarainen, Palonen, Paavola, & Lehtinen, 2004):

The Inquiry Framework

1. Develop an inquiry question. (What's your challenge of practice and why?)

2. Develop a working hypothesis and plan to investigate it. (How do you intend to intervene and why?)

3. Determine success criteria *and* associated evidence to be collected (and how).

4. Implement the plan.

5. Analyze the evidence in relation to the success criteria.

6. Reflect on the learning.

7. Determine "next practice" for the inquiry cycle to continue.

The inquiry process begins with the development of an inquiry question that is supported by evidence, followed by the formulation of a working hypothesis and a plan for investigating the hypothesis. The plan also includes determining success criteria and the associated evidence (how you will know if you've been successful). The plan is then implemented and the evidence is analyzed. The cycle is completed by reflection on the process (what did you learn?) and determination of "next practice" (where will you go next?).

While we don't disagree with this global process, we've learned a lot about the "high-frequency" implementation challenges that surround this process in leader learning contexts. As a result, we've been able to refine it in ways that support quality implementation. Our revised framework is modeled on the "plan, act, assess, reflect" professional learning cycle (Ontario Ministry of Education, 2011), but the key difference from the framework shown above is that the individual is not asked to plan for the entire inquiry at once, but instead to plan for one small learning move at a time. We see this as a more realistic and efficient way to engage in inquiry. Implementation unfolds one move at a time. The learning from one move leads to the plan for the next move, and so on. Our experience has shown us that building the plan, act, assess, reflect cycle into *each* learning move makes the inquiry more authentic. The updated framework looks like this:

The Revised Inquiry Framework

1. Develop an inquiry question. (What's your challenge of professional practice and why?)

2. Determine your "next best learning move." (How do you intend to intervene and why?)

For *each* "next best learning move":

1. Develop a plan to investigate the hypothesis.

2. Determine success criteria *and* associated evidence to be collected (and how).

(Continued)

(Continued)

3. Implement the plan.

4. Analyze the evidence in relation to the success criteria.

5. Reflect on the learning.

6. Determine "next practice" (the next "next best learning move") for the inquiry cycle to continue.

We have integrated this framework for planning, acting, assessing, and reflecting on discrete leadership learning moves into our inquiry template. The intent is for leaders, as they are moving through their inquiries and "making" learning moves, to intentionally and explicitly document what they are doing *and learning.* The "and learning" (rather than just the doing) is crucial here. Educators tend to be "action people." We get an idea and like to put that idea into action. Then, often before we're even done with the previous idea, we get the next idea and move forward on implementing that. In the language of the professional learning cycle, we're very good at "plan" and "act," but less so at "assess" and "reflect." In fact, we often find ourselves stuck in the cycle of plan-act, plan-act, plan-act, as we get excited to start the next move before taking the time to assess and reflect on what we learned from the previous one. This is problematic, because it is the assess and reflect components of the cycle that make it about learning. Without the assess and reflect, there is no learning, just doing. And worse, the unintended consequence is an assumption that it's good (or effective) doing. Assess and reflect give leaders what they need both to plan the next best learning move and to determine if the move is one worth repeating in the future.

Embedding the Professional Learning Cycle in Our Leadership Inquiry Template

We show how the professional learning cycle is embedded in our leadership inquiry template on page 108. Although the language in the second column refers to "My *next* best learning move," the first move a leader undertakes is obviously the "first" best learning move. Each move after that is the "next" best learning move, meaning the "best" thinking the leader can come up with about what to do next to better understand an aspect of the challenge of practice (i.e., to learn). (Note: The entire inquiry template for school leaders, including the questions described above that support getting to the inquiry question, appears at the end of this chapter p. 126, in Figure 5.1.)

Looking at this table in the template, the first thing that one might note is that three of the five columns are dedicated to planning the learning move. This demonstrates the importance that we place on the planning process. If the leader is not clear on the plan for the learning move (i.e., what he or she is hoping to learn, what he or she is specifically going to do to try to learn this, and how he or she is going to know if this learning has happened), then it will be impossible for him or her to assess and reflect on the learning move in a meaningful way. Additionally, the high degree of emphasis we place on the planning piece of the cycle is supported by the literature on expertise. Experts, regardless of domain, spend a significant amount of time planning—understanding what's needed and mapping out the requirements—before jumping into action (Glaser & Chi, 1988). Note also that each row of the template begins by asking the leader to articulate what he or she is hoping to learn with each move. This ensures that the leader is working on well-defined, specific goals, consistent with the research described in Chapter 4.

Using the first example provided in this chapter (of the principal of the midsize elementary school whose inquiry question was around learning how to influence teachers to take ownership over the PLC), we show the principal's first best learning move, as documented in her template on pages 109–110. Below the template illustration, we describe each column in detail.

Guiding Questions for the Next Best Learning Move

Plan	Plan	Plan	Assess	Reflect
What am I hoping to learn next?	My next best learning move: What *specifically* will I do to try to learn this?	How will I know if I have learned what I am hoping to learn? What conversation, observation, and/or product will I look at to know?	What happened? What did I find out when I considered those evidence sources?	What did I learn *from* this move? What did I learn *about* this move as a transferable intelligent leadership practice?

Example Principal's Next Best Learning Move

Plan	Plan	Plan	Assess	Reflect	
What am I hoping to learn next?	My next (first) best learning move: What *specifically* will I do to try to learn this?	How will I know if I have learned what I am hoping to learn? What conversation, observation, and/or product will I look at to know?	What happened? What did I find out when I considered those evidence sources?	What did I learn *from* this move?	What did I learn *about* this move as a potentially transferable intelligent leadership practice?
I want to learn if my hypothesis about people's connection to the PLC (that they don't feel connected to the learning) is right.	I will speak to 5 teachers (who seem disconnected from the PLC process) individually about their impressions about the learning happening in the PLC, by asking the following questions: 1. What have you learned in the PLC this year? 2. Do you see connections between the PLC work and your classroom practice (and, if so, specify)? 3. How do you think we could improve the PLC work?	Conversation: What teachers actually say Observation: How teachers respond to having this conversation with me (body language and attitude)	Although the teachers seemed to appreciate that I was asking their opinion, 4 of them that I spoke to seemed uncomfortable about having this conversation and said very little in response to my questions, though most of their comments were positive. (They said they do buy into the learning through the PLC.) The 5th person, who I have a good relationship with,	*From* the move: I got quite variable perspectives on the PLC. Despite the way I set up the conversations, I'm not sure the responses were honest. I'm wondering if those who were positive were all really telling the truth! I think I need to find another way to dig deeper around this . . . something anonymous maybe? *About* the move: The teachers seemed to appreciate being asked their opinion. When it comes to *building relationships and developing people*, I do think it's important to honor teachers' ideas and show respect for them, but I'm not

(Continued)

(Continued)

Plan	Plan	Plan	Assess	Reflect
What am I hoping to learn next?	My next (first) best learning move: What *specifically* will I do to try to learn this?	How will I know if I have learned what I am hoping to learn? What conversation, observation, and/or product will I look at to know?	What happened? What did I find out when I considered those evidence sources?	What did I learn *from* this move? What did I learn *about* this move as a potentially transferable intelligent leadership practice?
	I will explicitly tell them that I am having these conversations to learn how to better support them, and so I appreciate total honesty. I will also tell them that I am expecting some teachers to tell me that they don't feel very connected to the PLC work. My hope is that I will then get honest responses.		told me that while he respects the way I lead the PLC, he doesn't see it as authentic learning for him because he doesn't believe he has a learning need around mindset, and therefore, that he doesn't see it connected to his classroom practice.	sure this was the right way to do it in this circumstance. One-on-one discussions with teachers are probably useful in some circumstances, but maybe not here, given that I'm the one who leads the PLC and they might feel uncomfortable being honest with me given the power dynamic. Maybe I need to get this information in an anonymous way. I don't think I would do this specific move again. I would try one-on-one conversations again, but not where I was putting teachers on the spot to say what they are learning in a meeting that I lead.

In the first column, the leader is asked to articulate what specifically he or she is hoping to learn, or understand better, from this learning move. In the case of our example, the principal said: "I want to learn if my hypothesis about people's connection to the PLC (that they don't feel connected to the learning) is right." It is very important that the language of this column is in leader learning terms—in other words, that it contains an "I" learning statement. We sometimes see leaders completing this first column with statements such as "I want the teachers to . . ." It is essential to remember that leader learning moves are intended to be about what the *leader* wants to learn. This is not to say that influencing teacher practice isn't a valued outcome of a move, but the learning needs to be about the leadership practice that enables that outcome. For example, imagine that a school leader has an objective of influencing teachers around the organization of the manipulatives in their classrooms so they can be better used, and the leader proceeds with a hypothesis that giving teachers dedicated release time will enable this organization. Articulating the thinking in the first column of the template in terms of what the leader is hoping to learn from this move would look something like: "I want to learn if giving teachers dedicated release for a specific purpose gets them to organize manipulatives in their classrooms to make utilization more likely." Then, the actual "next best learning move"—as articulated in the second column of the template—describes specifically what giving teachers dedicated release time will look like. What we often see, however, is leaders interpreting and completing the first column of the template as a "happening"—what they want to happen. For instance, "I want teachers to organize the manipulatives in their classrooms." Unlike in the first example, there's no explicit leader learning intention articulated here. As we've said, a leadership inquiry is about learning to get better at influencing others. The core learning in this example is about the leadership practice of providing dedicated release time to shift teacher practice. While getting teachers to organize their manipulatives to better promote use is most certainly a worthwhile objective, it—in itself—isn't the point of the leadership learning inquiry.

In the second column of the template, the leader is asked to describe *specifically* the next best learning move that is intended to deliver on the learning outcome set out in the first column. The word *specifically* is crucial here, in that we are emphasizing the importance of the leader thinking through exactly what the move is going to look like in advance of making it. In the template example shown above, the principal's first learning move was about speaking to a few teachers to get their impressions about the learning happening in the PLC. However, defining the learning move as "I am going to speak to five teachers to get their impressions of the learning happening in the PLC" is not enough. What does "speak to" five teachers actually mean? It's quite conceivable that what actually gets said is where the real learning about influence will lie. And so the principal in our example articulated the details of the planned move by including the specific questions she intended to ask the five teachers individually. Leaders often find it challenging to plan a move with this degree of detail. We often hear things like "I'll have a conversation," but when the leader is pressed to unpack what having a conversation actually means, the details aren't there. Most of us can relate to the experience of knowing that we want to have a conversation with someone about something, but we leave it until we're actually in that conversation to decide specifically what we'll say. This is problematic because influence is subtle; it's often not that we have the conversation that makes the difference but the actual words we use. And from a transfer (or replication) perspective for both ourselves and our LLT colleagues, the real learning is in the details.

In the third column of the template, the leader articulates where he or she will look to assess the intended learning from the move. The leader specifies what conversation, observation, and/or product he or she will pay attention to. The principal who is asking five teachers about their impressions of the learning in the PLC to find out if she is correct in her hypothesis that people are disengaged will look to conversation (what the teachers actually say) as well as observation (how the teachers respond to having the conversation with her, in terms of both body language and attitude). The principal in the second example, who is planning to provide teachers with dedicated release time to see if it leads to a utilization-focused organization of classroom manipulatives, would look to observation (what the teachers do with the time they are given) and product (what the manipulatives look like afterward). The logic behind this column in the template is to prompt leaders to do advance thinking about what they will need to pay attention to in order to know if they learned what they hoped to.

Remember, the first three columns are all for *planning* the learning move and are thus contemplated in advance. Next, the leader makes the move, which is not on the template itself. The fourth column is the place for the leader to consider the evidence sources (from the third column) and describe what happened. This is the place for the first principal to say what she found out in terms of conversation and observation from those five teachers she had the one-on-one conversations with about the PLC work, or for the second principal to say what she observed the teachers doing with the dedicated release time and what the manipulatives in the classrooms looked like afterward. In all cases, the leader remains in the descriptive voice in this fourth column.

In the final column, the leader reflects on the learning in two ways. First, he or she responds to the question "What did I learn *from* this move?" This is a reflection on what was learned from making the move that will be used to move the inquiry forward—in other words, what was learned from this move that will direct the "next" best learning move? The first example principal reflected that she got variable perspectives on the PLC work and was left wondering whether the teachers were honest with her. She was left thinking that perhaps she needed to ask the same questions again using an anonymous forum and see whether that strategy might lead to more candor. This would presumably be her next best learning move (and in fact it was).

The second guiding reflection question, "What did I learn *about* this move as a transferable intelligent leadership practice?"

asks about broader implications of the move. It asks the leader to think about moving outside the petri dish of the particular inquiry and reflect on what he or she is learning that might be added to his or her tool kit of intelligent leadership practices. In fact, we encourage leaders to use the language of the intelligent leadership practices that we reviewed in Chapter 3 as categories for organizing the new knowledge they are building. This question asks for a reflection on the learning move itself. Was it a good move? Is it one worth repeating? The principal in our example reflected on her learning about the move by stating that although it's important to honor and respect teachers' ideas when it comes to "building relationships and developing people," and that one-on-one discussions might sometimes be useful for that, such one-on-one conversations might not be useful for soliciting candid responses when the person asking the questions holds a position of power and appears to have a vested interest in certain kinds of answers. The principal finished her reflection by saying that she wouldn't make this move again under similar circumstances. This is a learning that this principal will carry with her outside this particular inquiry.

In Chapter 4 we explained what it means to "get better" in terms of building more complex and sophisticated schemas or mental representations, and the role that trying something, failing at it, revising the strategy, and trying again plays in this process. For us, learning moves that don't work and won't be repeated are just as important as those that are successful and will be replicated. We often say that a failed "doing" move should be a successful "learning" move, and that's the whole purpose of inquiries. All moves are successful learning moves if we have been specific in our planning *and* if we "close the loop" by assessing and reflecting. The methodology of inquiry often doesn't yield immediate *best practice*, but it should always yield *next practice* (Katz & Dack, 2013). In fact, our own work has shown that the learning that grows out of initiatives (either teaching or professional learning initiatives) that have failed is a better predictor of changed practice than is learning that has grown out of successful initiatives (see Earl & Katz, 2006a). But as we have said elsewhere, the caveat is that we have to know that we failed and have the opportunity to think about why (Katz & Dack, 2013).

Small, Narrow, and Frequent Leadership Learning Moves

Our framework for successfully implementing the professional learning cycle hinges on planning, enacting, assessing, and reflecting on leadership learning moves that are small, narrow, and frequent. Having a planned conversation with a teacher, trying an activity at a staff meeting, sending an email in advance of a classroom or school visit, and reading a particular book or article are all examples of what we consider to be small, narrow learning moves. From our perspective, the intent of a leadership inquiry is for the leader to make his or her way through small, narrow learning moves like these, one at a time, carefully planning each move, executing the move, assessing what happened, and then reflecting on what has been learned in order to be able to define the next best learning move. In Chapter 4 we talked about the relationship between size and monitoring, in that the smaller the increments you're working in, the more likely you are to monitor (which is essential to closing the loop in inquiry).

Consider the following example of a learning move defined by a principal: "If I explicitly and directly ask Teacher A to share the journal activity she did with her Grade 3 class last week at our upcoming staff meeting, then I will learn if Teacher A is willing to share her work in front of her colleagues." This is a small, narrow move that requires the principal to simply ask a particular teacher one question in order to learn something. It's easy to monitor and reflect on. Once the principal completes the move, she can easily reflect on if she learned what she was hoping to learn, and what she will do next based on what she learned. Alternatively, if a move is large and multifaceted, it becomes very difficult to monitor. Imagine, for example, that this principal had said: "If I work with Teacher A and get her to share and collaborate with her colleagues, then other teachers will learn from her." While other teachers learning from this target teacher might be what the principal is ultimately after, the reality of influence is that it will require a number of smaller moves to get there. Grouping all the small pieces together into one large move makes it very difficult to monitor which parts of the move were successful and worth replicating. What does "work with" mean? What does "share and collaborate" mean?

In addition to smaller moves being significantly easier to monitor than larger ones, in Chapter 4 we also described the relationship between the size of the move and efficacy (the extent to which we feel that we are able to accomplish something). Essentially, the smaller the move, the more efficacious we feel—the more we feel that we are able to actually enact the move. And then in turn, the more efficacious we feel, the more likely we will be to monitor the move. We also referred to the psychology of "small wins," which essentially says that making small moves and learning from them helps to build momentum in an inquiry. All of this strongly suggests that making small, narrow, and frequent learning moves is the way to go, even though we're not very used to thinking and working in increments that are so small. Having one small, concrete goal at a time makes us feel like we are able to accomplish it, and that, in turn, makes us more likely to stick around to see how we did. And when we do accomplish it, we feel motivated to try to reach another goal. The inquiry templates of many of the leaders we work with are pages and pages long, made up of numerous small moves that unfold in a successive and sequential way as the leaders' understanding of influence grows deeper and they get better at leadership.

Below we share three more examples of next best learning moves that follow through all the columns on the template. In the first one, the school leader is engaging in an inquiry around learning how to influence the practice of a teacher who appears to be very resistant to change and with whom the school leader tends to have negative interactions. This example is of one small learning move that the school leader made in the inquiry.

Plan	Plan	Plan	Assess	Reflect
What am I hoping to learn next?	My next best learning move: What *specifically* will I do to try to learn this?	How will I know if I have learned what I am hoping to learn? What conversation, observation, and/or product will I look at to know?	What happened? What did I find out when I considered those evidence sources?	What did I learn *from* this move? What did I learn *about* this move as a transferable intelligent leadership practice?
I want to learn if Teacher A and I can have a positive professional interaction.	I will speak to Teacher A individually to learn more about her use of inquiry circles (what I see as her major strength that others can learn from), by specifically telling her that I am interested in hearing details about her inquiry circles because I think it's a strength that other teachers in the school can learn from.	Conversation: Teacher A's willingness to share details about her practice with me Observation: Teacher A's body language during the meeting (I will look at both as compared to how she usually acts when interacting with me.)	Teacher A seemed genuinely pleased that I was asking her about this. She described her practice in great detail and even showed me supporting resources. When I then suggested her sharing at a staff meeting, she was reluctant, stating that her colleagues don't value her opinion or practices, but that she would think about it.	*From* the move: I've never had such a productive conversation with her before. I think I need to let it sit a bit before I push about the staff meeting. I still need to figure out how to build from here to get her to think about changing her own practices. *About* the move: My one-on-one conversations with resisters usually have a much more negative tone. I think that what worked so well here is that I focused on a strength of hers, and I was explicit that I thought it was a strength. Maybe starting with a strength is a good place to begin in building a relationship with resisters, and once we have some foundation, we can move to talking about areas of growth.

The next example is of a small learning move that a school leader made as part of an inquiry that was focused on learning how to influence teachers to engage in learning that will improve practice around making student thinking visible in relation to proportional reasoning. In this example we show one of this leader's learning moves in detail across all five columns of the template, followed by the plan (the first three columns) of his subsequent next best learning move, to illustrate how the learning from one move leads into the plan for the next one.

The following example is of a small learning move made by a district superintendent who was working on an inquiry aimed at learning what aspects of her school visits help support the instructional leadership capacity of school leaders.

Why Sticking With the Template Matters

Earlier we mentioned that each leader working within a Leader Learning Team is engaging in his or her own leadership inquiry, using the collaborative group to help support his or her work. We will take up the collaborative group aspect of the LLT in Chapter 6. Each leader's individual inquiry is the work that lies at the heart of the LLT process, and the leadership inquiry template is intended to be a tool that supports that work. As we've seen, the overall purposes of the tool are (a) to ensure that the leadership inquiry question being worked on is just in time, job embedded, and needs based; and (b) to ensure that each next best learning move is fully processed as it follows through the cycle of plan, act, assess, reflect. The inquiry template should function as part of a leader's regular practice, as a "running record" of learning that continuously unfolds as the inquiry unfolds. The LLT meetings themselves are a check-in. They add an aspect of accountability to the leadership inquiry process (because of the social pressure), and—as we will see—they add value to the learning as the group provides critical feedback to support the inquiry.

Example Principal's Next Best Learning Move

Plan	Plan	Plan	Assess	Reflect
What am I hoping to learn next?	My next best learning move: What *specifically* will I do to try to learn this?	How will I know if I have learned what I am hoping to learn? What conversation, observation, and/or product will I look at to know?	What happened? What did I find out when I considered those evidence sources?	What did I learn *from* this move? What did I learn *about* this move as a transferable intelligent leadership practice?
I want to learn if staff (particularly those who have been resistant to change in math teaching) can understand the learning process that students go through and why it is important to provide multiple and varied opportunities for students to learn.	I will use a hands-on, experiential math activity at my staff meeting (i.e., staff have to do a similar task to what we expect of students). I will set up a mock grocery store, with a number of different stations, and working in groups, teachers will be asked to determine which product is the better deal.	Observation: I will observe staff reactions to the activity (e.g., are they engaged, do they seem to be considering proportional reasoning or the student learning experience in a way I haven't previously seen, etc.).	Most staff seemed to have some sort of "aha" moment. They reported things like "This was harder than I thought" and "I realized that hands-on opportunities are important."	*From* this move: Some of my fence-sitters seemed able to be swayed! There were a couple of people who I think will consider approaching teaching proportional reasoning differently now. I think I can move forward with some of these folks.

(Continued)

(Continued)

Plan	Plan	Plan	Assess	Reflect
What am I hoping to learn next?	My next best learning move: What *specifically* will I do to try to learn this?	How will I know if I have learned what I am hoping to learn? What conversation, observation, and/or product will I look at to know?	What happened? What did I find out when I considered those evidence sources?	What did I learn *from* this move? What did I learn *about* this move as a transferable intelligent leadership practice?
	For example, in one station I will provide two different packages of paper towels (different number of rolls in the packages, different size of rolls, different prices), and the teachers will have to figure out which makes more sense to buy. The full list of activities and questions is attached.[a] Teachers will work in groups of 3 or 4 and will rotate among the different stations.	Product: I will ask staff to briefly reflect on the experience at the end of the meeting in writing on an open-ended exit card.	There are still 2 obvious resisters (maybe more that are less obvious).	*About* this move: A hands-on, experiential activity is really good for a staff meeting. It was very successful for putting staff in the position of students. I would do this again!

a. This principal included his full list of questions/activities in a different file, so that column 2 of his template wouldn't get too long; we have not reproduced his full list here.

Plan	Plan	Plan	Assess	Reflect
What am I hoping to learn next?	My next best learning move: What *specifically* will I do to try to learn this?	How will I know if I have learned what I am hoping to learn? What conversation, observation, and/or product will I look at to know?	What happened? What did I find out when I considered those evidence sources?	What did I learn *from* this move? What did I learn *about* this move as a transferable intelligent leadership practice?
I want to learn if one particular Grade 4 teacher (call her Teacher X)—who was seemingly swayed during the staff meeting activity—will now be critically reflective of her current teaching around making thinking visible in relation to proportional reasoning. I want to see if she is able to make a distinction between her current practice and what she experienced in the simulation. I also want to know what support she needs.	I will have a one-on-one conversation with Teacher X, asking the following questions: 1. What have you been doing in your class around making thinking visible in relation to proportional reasoning? 2. How is this similar to or different from what you experienced during the simulation activity in the staff meeting? 3. How are you planning to move forward based on these reflections? 4. What support do you need to move forward in this way?	Conversation: What specifically Teacher X says		

Example Superintendent's Next Best Learning Move

Plan	Plan	Plan	Assess	Reflect
What am I hoping to learn next?	My next best learning move: What *specifically* will I do to try to learn this?	How will I know if I have learned what I am hoping to learn? What conversation, observation, and/or product will I look at to know?	What happened? What did I find out when I considered those evidence sources?	What did I learn *from* this move? What did I learn *about* this move as a transferable intelligent leadership practice?
I want to learn if the principal and I left the meeting during my school visit with a shared understanding of what the next steps are.	I will follow up my school visit by sending an email asking the principal to send me in writing what her next steps are so I can compare her understanding with my own.	Product: What the principal writes	The principal articulated almost the same next steps that I believe we had agreed on at the meeting. There was one piece that she left out that I responded with clarification on.	*From* the move: She and I seem to be on the same page about what we discussed at the meeting. When I responded with the piece she left out she apologized for forgetting about that, suggesting that leaving it out wasn't intentional. *About* the move: Asking the principal to provide me with a written summary of what we'd agreed on for next steps allowed me to ensure that we had a shared understanding and clarify anything that we weren't on the same page about. It also means that if she doesn't do what we agreed on we now have something in writing to go back to. I would definitely try this move again. I'm interested to see how it feels if I have an example of someone who provides me with a summary that looks very different from what I was expecting.

The real work of a leadership inquiry, however, happens between the LLT meetings, as the leaders enact their own inquiries using the template as a cognitive and behavioral scaffold, in an ongoing and regular way. In Chapter 4 we explained that focus and concentration are an integral part of improvement, yet they are difficult to maintain for long periods of time. Thus, shorter practice sessions with clear goals are more effective than longer ones. This is an important point when it comes to using the inquiry template. We have found that when leaders use the template regularly—to plan, act, assess, and reflect on a "row" once or twice a week—the result is much richer than when they work on the template only once a month (perhaps in preparation for the next LLT meeting). Human memory, regardless of how good people believe theirs to be, doesn't function like a video recorder (Woolfolk et al., 2015). Trying to "backfill" the template by "remembering" everything that was intended, done, and happened simply doesn't work!

It's a fairly frequent occurrence that our insistence on documenting learning in the template is met with a skeptical eye roll or some kind of verbal equivalent. We understand that "templates," in many school districts, are synonymous with the worst kind of activity traps (Katz et al., 2009). Beyond that, however, the discipline involved in the documentation requirement is effortful. But that's precisely why it's important. Purposeful practice, as we underscored in Chapter 4, is by definition effortful. That's why it works. Moreover, the exercise of "writing it down" is well supported by the research literature, not only because we are 42 percent more likely to *do* what we write down (Matthews, 2015) but also because of what's referred to as "knowledge transformation." Knowledge transformation is the way in which the writing process influences (or transforms) thought (Bereiter & Scardamalia, 1987). Often, when we struggle to write something down, it's because our thoughts aren't clear; getting the right words on the page requires that we do the right thinking in our heads. Good templates, in our view, are not simply recording spaces; they are tools for thinking.

KNOWING WHEN A LEADERSHIP INQUIRY IS "DONE"

A particular inquiry question does not remain at the center of a leader's professional learning forever. It endures for as long as the challenge of professional practice that sparked the inquiry continues to be an authentic learning space in which the leader can engage in purposeful practice directed at getting better at influence. This no longer being the case does not always correspond with the challenge or problem being "solved." Often leaders build momentum through learning moves such that they begin to feel that they know what they need to do. They might not have done it yet, but they know what to do. The inquiry has served its professional learning function, and it's time to move on. In other cases, as we alluded to earlier in this chapter, a challenge of practice may continue to be a place where the leader feels stuck, but the leader learns that the issue is a "one-off" when it comes to influence and is not really representative of a broader "class." Put slightly differently, the professional learning bang for the buck might not be there, so the leader chooses to move to a new inquiry question. In neither of the aforementioned cases does the leader's moving on mean that he or she is abandoning all work in relation to the challenge of practice. The work of leadership continues, while the focus for learning shifts. Remember the distinction we made earlier in this chapter between a learning focus and a *doing* focus; the leader always has a job to do that extends far beyond the narrow learning focus.

MOVING FORWARD

In this chapter we have explained the process of working to get better at influence by undertaking a leadership learning inquiry to deepen understanding, using our template as a tool for thinking. And while the work of purposeful practice is predominantly the responsibility of the individual leader looking to get better, it's not entirely a solitary pursuit. In Chapter 4, we described the potential value of collaborative learning communities. This gets at the "team" dimension of the Leader Learning Team. In the next chapter we describe the value added by the collaborative group as the members work together to analyze and provide feedback on each leader's individual inquiry. In particular, we highlight the Learning Conversations Protocol, which we use in LLTs to intentionally interrupt the "great discussions" that are sometimes seen in collaborative groups, in order to ensure real professional learning.

TIME FOR REFLECTION

1. Describe an adaptive challenge you are facing that is hindering your school improvement efforts.

2. What is your "next best learning move" to address this challenge, and what evidence will point to your learning?

3. How will you assess the impact of your "next best learning move" and then reflect on what you need to learn next?

Figure 5.1   The Inquiry Template for School Leaders

What are your school improvement priorities?

- Student learning foci:
  - Evidence (that this needs to be an area of focus for students):

- Teacher learning foci:
  - Evidence (that this needs to be an area of focus for teachers):

Where are you stuck as a leader in this school improvement process? On what, and with whom?

What leader learning opportunity does this define for you? (Your adaptive challenge defines your leadership inquiry question.)

- Inquiry question: How do I learn how to . . . ?

What's the transfer potential from your learning, in terms of intelligent leadership practices?

Plan	Plan	Plan	Assess	Reflect
What am I hoping to learn next?	My next best learning move: What *specifically* will I do to try to learn this?	How will I know if I have learned what I am hoping to learn? What conversation, observation, and/or product will I look at to know?	What happened? What did I find out when I considered those evidence sources?	What did I learn *from* this move? What did I learn *about* this move as a transferable intelligent leadership practice?

6

Ensuring That Together Is Better

In Chapter 5, we described the exercise of undertaking a leadership inquiry as an integral part of the Leader Learning Team (LLT) process. We explained how individual leaders engage in the process of inquiry to learn how to "get better" at *influence* as they work to enact intelligent leadership practices in responsive ways. In this chapter, we focus on the *T* in the LLT—that is, we consider the value added by the *team* aspect.

The Mechanics of the Leader Learning Team

The mechanics of the LLT are not complicated. Going through the motions is easy—it's the work that's hard. In an LLT, each leader individually works on his or her own inquiry by following the process described in Chapter 5. Then, every four to six weeks, for approximately two to three hours, the entire LLT (usually five or six individuals) meets. The meeting schedule is important. Meeting frequently helps build momentum for the individual inquiries and creates an accountability condition through regular timelines (e.g., "I want to get that learning move done before I share with my LLT next week"). It also ensures that there is a rhythm and regularity in how often the individual leadership inquiries come to the table. In a two- to three-hour focused meeting, three leaders usually have the chance to share and get feedback on their inquiries. With five or six people in an LLT, this usually means that an individual's inquiry makes it to the table every other meeting. Any less than that and momentum suffers. Ensuring that the meetings take place every four to six weeks and last two to three hours allows each individual's inquiry to make it to the table approximately every other month.

An LLT meeting is dedicated collaborative learning time with no distractions. It is important for every LLT to create and regularly review the members' own norms for working together as a group, including both norms for the work (what it means to come prepared, appropriate versus inappropriate discourse, and so on) and norms for minimizing distractions (whether using electronic devices during meetings is appropriate or not, how often to take breaks, and the like). While it might seem trivial to engage in explicit norm-setting around some of these things, our experiences with hundreds of LLTs suggest otherwise. For example, on several occasions we've witnessed groups whose members didn't think it necessary to set a norm about texting or emailing during the LLT meetings because "professionals know what is and isn't appropriate." Then, at the first meeting, one principal looks at her phone quite frequently, while others watch for an objection that doesn't come. At the next meeting, a few more do it ("If she can do it, why can't I?"). By the third meeting, all group members are distracted by their phones for a large portion of the time, and the quality of the learning suffers.

The Ongoing Spirit of Critical Friendship

The purpose of LLT meetings is for group members to act as "critical friends" to one another, to share their inquiries and what they are learning, and to receive critical feedback that pushes their thinking beyond what they could do on their own. Being in an LLT is about a culture of learning and an ongoing spirit of critical friendship. We introduced the notion of critical friendship earlier in this book, when we talked about the value of critical friends in helping us get outside our comfort zones and approach things from different perspectives. As the name implies, critical friends embody the qualities of both "critique" and "friendship." Critical friends work in the spirit of friendship, but they offer an open and honest critique of another person's beliefs and practices in a way that individuals often can't do alone (Baskerville & Goldblatt, 2009; Costa & Kallick, 1995; MacBeath, 1998). Critical friends can observe what may not be apparent to insiders, facilitate reflection on issues, ask questions, probe for justification and evidence to support perceptions, and help reformulate interpretations. What's key in the critical friend concept is that the appraisal that a critical friend provides is honest and challenging, yet with the purpose of being supportive and with an eye toward improvement. Critical friends don't tell you what you want to hear; they offer an external perspective that thwarts your tendency to seek only confirming evidence, as per the confirmation bias.

A culture of learning is about LLT members acting as critical friends to each other at all times, not just during the formal LLT meetings. Successful LLTs have structures in place to ensure that leaders are providing just-in-time critical friendship to one another in a needs-based way because it's sometimes not practical (or sensible) to wait for the next formal LLT meeting. Some groups, for example, regularly email one another between formal meetings. Others have critical friend pairs or triads that specify the "go-to" people for one another if they need support between meetings. The specific form of the between-meeting support is up to individual groups and can be changed on an ongoing basis as needs arise, but it is important to note that these "gap-filling" structures are intended to supplement, not replace, the formal LLT meetings. The formal LLT meetings are sacred. Not only do they create a space for what we call "learning on behalf of"—where the full group benefits from the learning of each individual (Katz et al., 2009)—but they also privilege the hard work of real learning through "intentional interruption" strategies. These conditions are difficult, if not impossible, to replicate in the informal settings of between-meeting support. In the remainder of this chapter, we describe what actually happens during formal LLT meetings in order to achieve these objectives.

OUR LEARNING CONVERSATIONS PROTOCOL: AN INTENTIONAL INTERRUPTION STRATEGY FOR ENHANCED COLLABORATIVE LEARNING

As we've said above, the purpose of LLT meetings is for leaders to share their inquiries and what they are learning and to receive critical feedback that pushes their thinking beyond where they can get to on their own. While this is easy to state in theory, successful implementation in practice is much more elusive. In Chapter 4, we described the research that demonstrates how a collaborative setting can add value to the work of an individual in terms of building *deep understanding*—the necessary requirement for "getting better." But we also highlighted the much more likely default practices of collaboration that work as impediments to doing just this. Just because a group gets together for the well-intentioned purpose of learning doesn't automatically ensure that any real learning will take place. We described the "great discussions" that we have observed time and time again in collaborative settings; encounters are filled with agreement, confirmation, little diversity of opinion, and little focus on how the discussion will translate into next steps in learning. We then went on to describe the value of protocols in helping a group to intentionally interrupt "great discussions" (which result in little learning) and move toward "focused learning conversations" (which are planned and systematic, with an emphasis on building deep understanding). We developed our Learning Conversations Protocol to help Leader Learning Teams achieve this objective. LLT meetings have no other agenda items beyond the structured learning conversations guided by the protocol (regardless of how tempting it might be for members to use this "together" time to talk about other issues of mutual interest or concern). Maintaining this dedicated purpose and focus is paramount.

This protocol, like most others, requires someone to take responsibility for actively facilitating the process. Active facilitation ensures that people follow the instructions and complete each step of the protocol as specified. Since the protocol requires participants to behave in ways that aren't natural (and the protocol only exists for that reason), without an active facilitator groups often revert to the default practices that the protocol is intended to interrupt. Actively facilitating the protocol is a skill that requires practice. The facilitator needs to know and understand the protocol well enough to recognize when there's a deviation, as well as when and how to intervene when this is happening. Over time, the goal would be for LLT group members to rotate the facilitation role among themselves, as each individual becomes more skilled in the process. In addition to the role of facilitator, there is always one person who is the presenter (referred to in the protocol as the "leader presenter"). All other group members act as critical friend analysts/feedback providers. Earlier in this chapter we described the potential of critical friendship and outlined the role of critical friend as an important relationship function for LLT members. But it's important to underscore that neither being a critical friend nor benefiting from having a critical friend is easy. Simply calling people "critical friend analysts" certainly does not guarantee that they will behave in ways that are consistent with that label. Remember that the culture of "superfice" (superficial niceness) is always working in the background, and it is compelling. And at the same time, having a critical friend, even one fighting against the culture of superfice and providing honest feedback, doesn't guarantee receptivity to the critique; the person receiving the feedback must *want* to hear it. The Learning Conversations Protocol is intended to put a structure in place that helps LLT members behave in ways that allow for the promise of critical friendship to be fully realized.

Below we describe each section of the protocol in detail, one section at a time. (The complete protocol is displayed at the end of this chapter in Figure 6.1, pp. 154–155.) For each section, we include discussion of its conceptual underpinnings— that is, an explanation of why that piece of the protocol is important. We intentionally describe the protocol in this way. Tools (like this protocol) tend to travel more readily than their conceptual underpinnings. The problem is that when a tool is implemented without a strong understanding of the "why" behind it, it often fails. We have seen numerous examples of people who have begun to use this protocol and made "tweaks" to it because they didn't understand why particular components exist. And the result was that they "tweaked out" all of the intentionality behind the protocol! That's when a protocol has the potential to become an "activity trap"— something that is well-intentioned but is not needs based and therefore not a productive use of time or resources (Katz et al., 2009). It is essential that the protocol and the "why" behind each component are kept together, because the "why" is the key to successful facilitation (and implementation). You'll see that explicating the "why" is built into the protocol directly, as the facilitator explains the rationale behind each section throughout the process.

After describing each section of the protocol in detail, we also provide example text from a real LLT meeting to illustrate what the protocol looks like "in action." As with Chapter 5, while we focus on a Leader Learning Team made up of *school* leaders in this chapter, other leader teams (such as district leaders and teacher leaders) regularly use the protocol as well.

SETTING THE STAGE FOR THE PROTOCOL

- Facilitator to review the norms as well as the "why" behind them:
  - ○ Follow the steps
  - ○ No placing blame
  - ○ Tolerate discomfort in the process
  - ○ Leader presenter to take his or her own notes
  - ○ Everyone else to keep a parking lot for personal connections (aka be selfish!)

Prior to beginning with the protocol, the facilitator reviews the process and the norms for the protocol, as well as the "why" behind the norms. The instructions of following the steps, not placing blame, and the leader presenter taking his or her own notes are fairly self-explanatory at this point, but there are two norms that we need to describe in greater detail. First, the norm of "tolerating discomfort in the process" is especially important. As mentioned, a protocol like this is uncomfortable by design. You will see as you read below that there are a number of components of the process that would be quite uncomfortable for someone not used to it. One of the criteria for successful implementation of the protocol is tolerating this discomfort. Comfort cannot be a success criterion for using the protocol effectively, as discomfort is an essential prerequisite for real (permanent) new learning. Recall that in Chapter 4 we highlighted getting outside one's comfort zone as one of the most important aspects of purposeful practice. We have observed groups who have said things like "We really didn't like the way it felt to do it that way, so we made a change that was more comfortable for our group." While that might sound commendable, it's actually problematic, because making a change to make the protocol "more comfortable" likely means allowing behaviors that the protocol was designed to intentionally interrupt! That's why sticking to the protocol is a norm, as is tolerating the discomfort that comes along with that.

Another norm that is important to describe here is the one concerning keeping a "parking lot for personal connections." This norm asks that all group members, while participating in a collaborative analysis of someone else's work by acting as critical friend analysts/feedback providers, also keep a "parking lot" for the connections that they are making to their own practice. The parking lot norm ensures that all participants leave the meeting having explicitly labeled how their own thinking has been pushed and how they might move their own learning forward, whether they were a leader presenter that day or not. We always tell people that using the protocol is about both benevolence and selfishness. It's important to come to these learning encounters with the goal of helping colleagues move forward in their work. But there must be a selfish component as well, in that all group members must leave the learning encounter feeling that they have learned something for themselves. The parking lot for personal connections helps to create accountability for individual learning and intentionally interrupts the notion of diffusion of responsibility described in Chapter 4.

---

1. INTRODUCTION

(5–8 minutes)

- The facilitator reviews the "why" behind this step.
- Leader presenter to briefly explain where he or she is in the process—leadership inquiry, last few next best learning moves, reflections (learning "from" and "about" the moves)—using his or her updated inquiry template as support.

In the first step of the protocol (5–8 minutes), the leader presenter shares his or her work, including the inquiry question and the evidence for it, the learning moves that he or she has been making, and the learning that has emerged from them. When the presenter is just beginning with his or her inquiry, it might be the case that only the first page of the template has been completed (i.e., no learning moves have been made yet), and the presenter is looking for feedback on whether the inquiry question is an authentic learning need, or what learning move to try first, or something else about the inquiry question itself. In subsequent meetings where this same person is presenting and the group is familiar with the leadership inquiry being presented, the presenter does not start back at the beginning of the template. Instead, he or she reminds the group of the inquiry question and why this is a challenge of practice for him or her, updates the group on what work he or she has done since the last time that inquiry was presented, and articulates where he or she is currently feeling stuck.

When sharing the details of learning moves that have been completed, presenters should spend most of their time describing the first column (what they wanted to learn from the move), the second column (specifically what they did), and the fifth column (what they learned from and about the move). While everything documented on the template is important, the maximum time allowed for this section is 8 minutes, and 8 minutes goes by fast, hence the need to prioritize. We find it very useful for the presenter to provide copies (either electronic or hard copies) of his or her template for LLT members, so that they are able to *see* the template rather than just hear it being described. This allows them to look at additional details on their own, review the template at their own pace, go back as needed, and note the exact language being used (which is often important and becomes a topic of discussion). Some groups choose to share their templates with one another electronically in advance of each meeting, so group members have time to look them over.

You can see how pivotal the leader presenter's inquiry template is to the Learning Conversations Protocol—and we don't just mean the artifact, but the inquiry itself.

The protocol is a processing mechanism that works only if it has something to process. The better the quality of what it has to process, the more value it can add. But it can't make something out of nothing. Quality output requires quality input. In other words, the leader presenter must bring his or her best thinking to the table to get the most out of the Learning Conversations Protocol.

The parameters set out for this first section of the protocol, including the time limit, are designed to intentionally interrupt the propensity that people have to tell long stories, rather than to be concise, when given the opportunity to "present." Having to share the template in a maximum of 8 minutes ensures that the presenter focuses only on the details that are necessary for the group to understand the work being undertaken.

Below we provide an excerpt from a real Leader Learning Team meeting. The leader presenter in this sample is the principal whose inquiry appeared as the main example in Chapter 5: the principal of the midsize elementary school whose inquiry question was around learning how to influence teachers to assume ownership over the professional learning community (PLC), where they were learning about growth mindset in relation to mathematics. This example is followed throughout this chapter as well, and the excerpts shown are from the second time this principal shared her inquiry with her LLT. As you follow this example throughout this chapter, remember that we are not providing a full transcript of each section of the learning conversation (which space does not permit), but rather illustrative excerpts.

Excerpt From Protocol Step 1

Leader presenter: Last time I shared my work with you I described how I developed my inquiry question. You can read the first page of my template in detail, so I'll just briefly remind you. My teacher learning focus is on learning strategies for changing student mindset in math, and we have been working on this in the PLC all year. My problem, and where I'm feeling stuck, is that I don't feel like most of the teachers in the school are taking ownership over their professional learning. I feel like I alone own this. And I have no idea how to move forward. So my inquiry question is: How do I learn how to lead people who might not feel personally connected to the PLC and get them to take ownership over the learning?

Since I presented last month I've completed my first learning move and planned my second one. The first move took me a couple of weeks to do since it involved speaking privately to five different teachers. I made this move because I wanted to learn if my hypothesis about people's connection to the PLC, that they don't feel connected to the learning, is correct. So I chose 5 teachers who I think are disconnected from the PLC process, and I had one-on-one conversations with them. I specifically asked 3 questions: What have you learned in the PLC this year?; Do you see connections between the PLC work and your classroom practice, and if so, to specify?; and How do you think we could improve the PLC work? I also want to mention that I told them that I was having these conversations to learn how to better support them, and that I really wanted complete honesty. I also told them that I was expecting some teachers to tell me that they don't feel very connected to the PLC work. This was an attempt to encourage them to really be honest and know that I would be okay with and truly appreciate whatever they told me.

But I'm not sure my approach worked! You can read the details, but you'll see that 4 of the 5 gave me little information, and only positive responses. They seemed uncomfortable having the conversation with me. One teacher, who I have a good relationship with, told me that the PLC is not authentic learning for him. So what I learned *from* this move is that despite the way I set up the conversations, I'm not sure the responses were honest. I'm wondering if those who were positive were all really telling the truth. I decided I needed to find another way to dig deeper around this, like something anonymous, and you'll see in a minute that this is my plan for my next learning move. I learned a few things *about* this move specifically. First of all, the teachers seemed to appreciate that I cared about their opinion, but they seemed to not like having the one-on-one conversation with me. When it comes to building relationships, I do think it's important to honor teachers' ideas and show respect for them, but I'm not sure this was the right way to do it. One-on-one discussions with teachers are probably useful in some circumstances, but maybe not here, given that I'm the one who leads the PLC and they might feel uncomfortable being honest with me given the power dynamic, which is why I'm planning something anonymous for my next move. I wouldn't repeat this particular move again in the future. I would try one-on-one conversations again, but in different circumstances, not where I am putting teachers on the spot to say what they are learning in a meeting that I lead.

So in terms of my next best learning move, I really still have the same thing I want to learn, which is whether my hypothesis about people's lack of ownership over the PLC is right—because I still feel like I don't know the answer. So my plan is to ask these same questions to all teachers in the school, in an anonymous forum this time. I am getting the electronic survey together this week . . . also a new learning for me! . . . and I hope to send it out to teachers by Monday.

2. CLARIFYING THE LEADER PRESENTER'S WORK

(5–8 minutes)

- The facilitator reviews the "why" behind this step.
- The group asks clarifying questions to fill in any gaps.
- The group offers no judgments or interpretations about what the leader presenter was doing, and no suggestions.
- Leader presenter answers specific questions in a crisp and precise manner.

In the second step of the protocol (5–8 minutes), the group asks clarifying questions to fill in any gaps in what was presented in Step 1. Clarifying questions are those that the presenter can easily answer. They don't have to be yes/ no questions, but they do need to be answered crisply and precisely. They shouldn't require the presenter to give them much thought in order to arrive at answers. Examples of clarifying questions include "What grade are you referring to?"; "How many teachers are in the math department?"; "What specific questions did you ask at that meeting?"; and "Was this the first time that group worked together?" The intent of this section of the protocol is to ensure that the group has a complete picture of what has been presented while putting limits on the presenter's typical temptation to pontificate (because the presenter is allowed only to answer the questions, and not say more). In addition, this section of the protocol is designed to intentionally interrupt the propensity that people have to listen to a presentation and quickly make it about themselves, saying something like "That once happened to me when. . . ." Allowing only clarifying questions from the critical friends at this point ensures that the group focuses exclusively on understanding what the presenter has shared.

Excerpt From Protocol Step 2

Critical friend A: Remind me how many teachers you have?

Leader presenter: Twenty-six.

Critical friend B: Can you tell me a bit about the teachers you spoke to in your first move?

Leader presenter: There was no particular profile. I tried to choose teachers who were different from each other. Except that I didn't choose anyone who I have no relationship with whatsoever because I thought it would be too uncomfortable. Let me think . . . Two of them have been at the school more than ten years. One has been here about five years. The other two are new teachers in the last couple years. I have a closer relationship with one than the others.

Critical friend C: When did these one-on-one meetings happen, and did the teachers know in advance what you'd be asking about?

Leader presenter: During prep periods, and no, they didn't know in advance.

3. INTERPRETING THE LEADER PRESENTER'S WORK

(8–10 minutes)

- The facilitator reviews the "why" behind this step.
- The group tries to understand the leadership inquiry and/or latest learning move(s) at a deeper level.
- Each individual puts forward how he or she is conceptualizing or representing what the group has heard.
- Group members avoid any push to consensus and put forward as many different ways of thinking about the inquiry as possible.
- Group members offer no suggestions.
- Possible prompts:
  - "I think I heard/didn't hear [leader presenter] say that . . ."
  - "This makes me think about . . ."
  - "I wonder if this issue is really about . . ."
  - "I am curious why [leader presenter] would think that . . ."
  - "I wonder what assumptions [leader presenter] is making in order to draw those conclusions . . ."
- Leader presenter:
  - Doesn't speak, listens to how he or she has been understood by the group.
  - Asks him- or herself, "Why would they think that?"
  - Works on active listening—agree before you disagree. Asks him- or herself, "Why might they be right?"

In the third and possibly most pivotal section (8–10 minutes), the group (other than the presenter) works together to try to understand the presenter's inquiry and learning at a deeper level. The intent is for the group to put forward as many different ways of thinking about the work as possible, rather than come to consensus. This interrupts the propensity for groupthink. In addition, because diversity of ideas rather than agreement is the expectation, group members are encouraged specifically to speak up if they disagree with an interpretation made by another critical friend.

Importantly, no suggestions are allowed in this step, which is contrary to what people tend to do when left to their own devices. This section is about ensuring a push to a "deeper understanding" of the challenge, which, as we described in Chapter 4, is a hallmark practice of expertise. The rationale is that when suggestions are made later (in Step 5 of the protocol), they are better and more refined as a result of the commitment to deep understanding in this step.

Note that the presenter is not permitted to speak in this section of the protocol. Instead, he or she is asked to engage in active listening, practicing what we call "agree before you disagree," while keeping his or her own notes. This is intended to be an interruption of the natural inclination that people have to be defensive as the confirmation bias is encouraging them to explain away any challenging feedback they're hearing. Further, forcing the presenter to actively listen and remain silent serves as an opportunity for the presenter to engage in a priority-setting exercise. In "great discussions," points that are raised early often dictate the flow of the discussion even if they're not most important. Here, forced and active listening creates space for the presenter to mentally sort what is said based on what resonates the most. Active listening has been identified as one of the most important, yet underdeveloped, leadership skills (Cowan, 2015).

We have found that in Step 3 (and later in Step 5), when the presenter is not permitted to speak, it works well for the rest of the group to refer to the presenter in the third person, almost as if he or she were not present, and to avoid eye contact with the presenter. While this inevitably feels strange at first, it makes it easier for the presenter to inhibit the desire to react, either verbally or nonverbally. Moreover, if the setup of the room is conducive, we also suggest that the presenter push back from the table and "retreat into" his or her notes during Steps 3 and 5.

Critical friend B: I am curious about the teacher who [leader presenter] believes was honest with her and who [leader presenter] said she has a good relationship with. This teacher said the PLC isn't authentic learning for him. What is his attitude toward professional learning like? Does he *want* the PLC to be an authentic learning opportunity for him? What I mean is, does he want to learn?

Critical friend D: I am wondering what [leader presenter] is planning to say to teachers when she sends out the survey. I think this will really set the tone for how people approach the survey.

Critical friend C: I was thinking the same thing. I didn't hear [leader presenter] say anything about what the email will say when she sends the message out, or if she's going to say anything to teachers about this in person, and I was wondering if she's thought about it.

Critical friend A: I am wondering if [leader presenter] could end up in the same situation after doing her next learning move with the email survey. Will she truly get honesty with the survey? Do you think the teachers will still tell her what they think she wants to hear?

Critical friend E: They might, but I'm not sure she has a better way to do it. This is already anonymous, what else can she do? But it does reiterate the importance of [leader presenter] thinking about how she's going to present this to teachers. . . . I think she needs to—[interrupted by facilitator]

Facilitator:	Remember, no suggestions yet.
Critical friend E:	Oops. [laughter]
Critical friend A:	I'm starting to wonder if it's appropriate to be asking these questions of teachers at all, even in an anonymous survey. I think this puts them in an uncomfortable position and isn't fair to them.
Critical friend C:	I disagree. Let's think back to the purpose of this. [Leader presenter] wants to make the PLC an authentic learning experience for teachers so that people take ownership over their learning. How can she do that without knowing where they're starting from? Maybe her thinking is totally wrong! Her whole inquiry hinges on her getting these questions answered as honestly as possible.
Critical friend D:	I agree with [Critical friend C]. The questions she's asking really aren't putting people on the spot in any way, especially in an anonymous forum. Having to answer her face-to-face is different, and she already learned that didn't work well! But I think what she's doing here is okay, and is actually important to do.

4. QUICK CLARIFICATION

(2 minutes)

- The facilitator reviews the "why" behind this step.
- Group members ask any additional questions of clarification that have come up.
- Leader presenter can clear up any inaccuracies or missing information (but not more than that).

In the fourth section (maximum of 2 minutes), the group members have the opportunity to ask any last clarification questions that have come up and that they need answered prior to making suggestions (in Step 5). This additional clarification section is included because it is often the case that the interpretation conversation in Step 3 leads to additional questions of clarification that the group wishes had been asked earlier. Importantly, this section is a *quick* clarification. In addition to the group asking any last clarification questions, the presenter is permitted to clear up any inaccuracies that were heard (i.e., if the group misunderstood something), but is not allowed to say more. This continues to be an interruption of the presenter's propensity to want to defend and confirm without thinking through the feedback. Without being explicitly reminded that only factual inaccuracies can be cleared up here, the presenter tends to start to respond to everything said in Step 3. This step sometimes takes no time at all because it's often the case that no one has any further clarification questions and nothing was misunderstood.

Excerpt From Protocol Step 4

Critical friend E: Have you thought about how you are going to present the survey to the teachers?

Leader presenter: No.

---

5. IMPLICATIONS FOR THINKING (AND PRACTICE)

(8–10 minutes)

- The facilitator reviews the "why" behind this step.
- Group members discuss the implications for the leader presenter's learning or where they think the leader presenter

(Continued)

(Continued)

should go next in his or her thinking based on what they've heard and discussed.

- Possible prompts:
  - "I think [leader presenter] really might want to think about . . ."
  - "I think a possible next step in [leader presenter's] learning might be . . ."
  - "Is there other evidence that can be gathered around . . . ?"
  - "What do you think about [leader presenter] trying to learn . . . ?"
- Leader presenter doesn't speak and works on active listening.

Step 5 of the protocol (8–10 minutes) is for suggestions, which feedback providers usually like. This is the place where the critical friends get to say what they think should happen next! What's important, however, is that the critical friend analysts make suggestions that are informed by the interpretive work that was previously done on deeply understanding the presenter's inquiry. Also, notice that the language of the protocol indicates that the group is to make suggestions for the presenter's *learning* (and thinking), rather than activity; the distinction is important, given that an inquiry is intended to be focused on learning. This is an intentional interruption of the propensity of human beings to focus on action ("doing") rather than on learning or thinking. Again, the presenter is not permitted to speak in this section, for the same reasons as in Step 3.

Excerpt From Protocol Step 5

Critical friend E: I think that how [leader presenter] presents this survey to the teachers is crucial. She needs to figure out how to get the most honest responses. I think that when she sends out the survey she needs to write a message that sounds a lot like what she said to the teachers when she initially asked them in person; that she fully expects some teachers to say they don't feel connected to the PLC.

Critical friend A: I think she needs to go further than that. I think she needs to say exactly why she's asking this. Something like "I suspect the PLC is not feeling authentic and connected to your classroom for some of you, and I want to learn how to change that, and that's why I'm asking this."

Critical friend D: I actually think she should talk to teachers about this in person. I don't think they should hear about it for the first time through email. They might have questions. And we know how well some people read their email! [laughter]

Critical friend B: Good point. In person is a good idea.

Critical friend C: I have a completely different suggestion from what we've been talking about. I think she should make a learning move that's focused on learning more about the teacher she already spoke to, the one she believes she got an honest response from and already has a good relationship with. Is there more to learn from this teacher? Can this teacher help [leader presenter] move forward in any way? They've already started down this path together as a result of the conversation they had, so why not follow up with it?

6. CONSOLIDATE THINKING AND PLAN NEXT STEPS

(5 minutes)

- The facilitator reviews the "why" behind this step.
- Leader presenter refers to his or her notes and summarizes what he or she is thinking (with input from the group). What resonates?
- If possible, leader presenter talks about the next best learning move.

In this step, the group gives the floor back to the presenter, who has the opportunity to talk about what is resonating with him or her based on what he or she has heard. This section is not meant to be an inventory of responses to everything that has been said, but rather a "think aloud." As mentioned above, human beings tend not to be natural thinkers, and instead prefer to "do." This section is intended to interrupt that by creating a space for thinking and for the presenter to articulate publicly what he or she is going to think and learn about next, and why. Presenters sometimes find it difficult to articulate a specific next best learning move at this point, given that they sometimes need time to digest the feedback before they can determine what they want to learn about next. However, if they have ideas about their next best learning move(s), they are asked to share them here.

Speaking in this section of the protocol is not restricted to the presenter. Others do speak where relevant and appropriate, but the presenter takes the lead. For example, if the presenter has a question or a thought about a comment or suggestion that was made previously, it can be followed up here. Ultimately, the leader presenter owns and takes responsibility for his or her own learning. There is no obligation or requirement to take up any of the proffered suggestions. The opportunity is intended to provide a richer sounding board for the leader presenter's own thinking.

Leader presenter:	First of all, thank you very much for this. I was sitting and listening to you and thinking I can't believe that I didn't think about how I was going to present the survey to the teachers. I was just going to send it out next week and ask teachers to do it, so I'm really glad we had this meeting first! I'm realizing that what I say is really important, and I agree that in person is a good idea. We have a staff meeting on Wednesday, so maybe I can talk about it then and answer any questions, and then send it out. I have to think more about what exactly I will say. I don't know if I want to tell them that I am trying to learn how to make the PLC more authentic for them. I see the benefit of saying that, but it also feels risky. What if I fail at it? I have to think about that more. Maybe I will touch base with one of you in the next few days to run my plan for exactly what I'm going to say by you. But what I realize is I definitely need to say something in advance to give myself the best shot at learning what I want to learn. I can't just send the survey out!

7. REFLECTIONS ON THE PROCESS

(5–8 minutes)

- The facilitator reviews the "why" behind this step.
- Leader presenter reflects on his or her learning from the collaborative analysis by being asked: How did we push your thinking and add value because we were together?

(Continued)

(Continued)

- Each member of the group shares one thing that was put in his or her "parking lot" of personal connections.
- The whole group reflects on the process of using the protocol (what did/didn't work well in terms of the intended "learning conversation" objective).

In the final step of the protocol, the leader presenter is asked how his or her thinking was pushed and how value was added as a result of the group's working through the protocol together. Each group member then specifically articulates how his or her own thinking was pushed by sharing something from his or her "parking lot" of personal connections. The personal accountability required here ensures that participants maintain their individual identities within the group, as well as each take personal responsibility for the learning. This is again an intentional interruption, of both groupthink and diffusion of responsibility. Finally, the group reflects on using the protocol itself, as well as on the learning. Here the group self-assesses against the intention of the protocol (to push thinking beyond what people would be able to achieve on their own) to ensure that the objective was met. If the objective was not met, the group discusses what didn't work and why, in the service of better learning for the next time.

Reflecting on using the protocol is an essential part of the process. It is often tempting for groups to shortchange or even skip this last step, in the interest of "moving on" and getting to the next leader presenter. This is particularly tempting with groups who have been working together for some time and assume the protocol is always "working." Sometimes this group familiarity translates into becoming lax with the active facilitation requirement, and fidelity to the process becomes loose. This reflection on the process doesn't need to take long because there's often little to say, but in our experience it's important to make a deliberate space for it.

In the example we've been following through in this chapter, the leader presenter reiterated that her thinking was pushed as a result of the group's working together because what she was now planning to think about next—how to best set up the survey to give her a good shot at actually learning what she hopes to—hadn't been in the forefront of her mind prior to this meeting. The reflections on using the protocol were also fairly straightforward during this meeting. The group members felt that the protocol achieved its objective, and they did not have anything they felt they needed to change moving forward. The excerpt provided below comes from the parking lot connections of some of the group members.

Excerpt From Protocol Step 7

Critical friend B: I'm thinking about the way a teacher perceives the power differential between themselves and their principal . . . it can be huge. I think I put teachers on the spot all the time, asking them questions they might not be comfortable answering honestly. But how am I supposed to get this information in a way that doesn't put them on the spot? We can't always do an anonymous survey.

Critical friend A: I'm really curious about the teacher that [leader presenter] has started down the path with, and I'm thinking more about [critical friend C's] suggestion of following up with him. I have a teacher on my staff who is often honest with me in this way. I used to think it was helpful because she would give me "intel" but I'm starting to realize that this "intel" is almost always negative. She likes to talk and she likes that she and I have a good relationship, but I don't know that she likes to learn.

Critical friend E: My parking lot connection is that I just think that what [leader presenter] is trying to learn about is so interesting. What she learns about how to create the conditions for a truly authentic PLC is going to be so useful for all of us. Think about it: We all talk about "the PLC" when we really mean "the formal meeting where we do our professional learning." If teachers don't own the learning, is it really even a PLC? I can't imagine that there's anyone here who isn't experiencing this same challenge at least to some degree.

Taken together, the seven steps of the Learning Conversations Protocol serve a collaborative group process that adds value to the work of an individual. Using this protocol constitutes the entire agenda of LLT meetings; group members rotate sharing their inquiry work with their colleagues in order to gain critical feedback and ideas for next steps in their learning. In a two- or three-hour LLT meeting, where three different leaders are sharing their inquiries, the protocol would be repeated three times. Groups come to learn how to use the protocol fairly quickly, gaining comfort with the process of the learning conversation.

TOWARD A PREFERRED FUTURE OF THE INTELLIGENT, RESPONSIVE SCHOOL

In this book, we have outlined a preferred future in which the tension between perceived opposites can actually be a productive force on the road toward enhanced professional learning and improved practice. When schools are intelligent, they provide clear evidence and research-informed direction to the professionals in the building. When schools are responsive, they understand the unique circumstances in each learning space that must be honored so that while the work is informed by intelligent expectations, implementation is guided by contextual familiarity. Leading these kinds of intelligent, responsive schools requires intelligent, responsive leadership practice. And this kind of leadership capacity takes work to develop. Research on "strategic execution" reminds us that improvement efforts often fail, not because of the quality of the ideas, but because of challenges with their implementation (McChesney et al., 2012). It's not enough just to know what the effective leadership practices are. Building a deep understanding of *how* to enact these leadership practices in a particular context in order to "influence" improvement is where the real work (and professional learning) for leaders lies. We've explained the process of working to get better at influence by undertaking leadership learning inquiries to deepen understanding. And we've argued that while this work—which takes the form of purposeful practice—is predominantly the responsibility of the individual leader, collaborative learning communities can make "together better than alone" by adding value through focused learning conversations.

TIME FOR REFLECTION

1. Who are your critical friends and how have they helped you improve your practice?

2. How impactful are the learning teams in which you participate, and what ideas do you now have to improve them?

3. How "intelligent" and "responsive" is your school, and how will you use the insights you gained from this book to support learning and leading?

Figure 6.1   The Learning Conversations Protocol

Protocol roles: 1 facilitator (rotating) 1 leader presenter Everyone else: critical friend analysts/feedback providers

Setting the Stage for the Protocol
 	
• Facilitator to review the norms as well as the "why" behind them:
  ○ Follow the steps
  ○ No placing blame
  ○ Tolerate discomfort in the process
  ○ Leader presenter to take his or her own notes
  ○ Everyone else to keep a parking lot for personal connections (aka be selfish!)

1. Introduction (5–8 minutes) • The facilitator reviews the "why" behind this step. • Leader presenter to briefly explain where he or she is in the process—leadership inquiry, last few next best learning moves, reflections (learning "from" and "about" the moves)—using his or her updated inquiry template as support.
2. Clarifying the Leader Presenter's Work (5–8 minutes) • The facilitator reviews the "why" behind this step. • The group asks clarifying questions to fill in any gaps. • The group offers no judgments or interpretations about what the leader presenter was doing, and no suggestions. • Leader presenter answers specific questions in a crisp and precise manner.

3. Interpreting the Leader Presenter's Work (8–10 minutes)
 	
• The facilitator reviews the "why" behind this step.
• The group tries to understand the leadership inquiry and/or latest learning move(s) at a deeper level.
• Each individual puts forward how he or she is conceptualizing or representing what the group has heard.
• Group members avoid any push to consensus and put forward as many different ways of thinking about the inquiry as possible.
• Group members offer no suggestions.
• Possible prompts:
  ○ "I think I heard/or didn't hear [leader presenter] say that . . ."
  ○ "This makes me think about . . ."
  ○ "I wonder if this issue is really about . . .'"
  ○ "I am curious why [leader presenter] would think that . . ."
  ○ "I wonder what assumptions [leader presenter] is making in order to draw those conclusions . . ."

- Leader presenter:
  - Doesn't speak, listens to how he or she has been understood by the group.
  - Asks him- or herself, "Why would they think that?"
  - Works on active listening—agree before you disagree. Asks him- or herself, "Why might they be right?"

4. Quick Clarification (2 minutes)

- The facilitator reviews the "why" behind this step.
- Group members ask any additional questions of clarification that have come up.
- Leader presenter can clear up any inaccuracies or missing information (but not more than that).

5. Implications for Thinking (and Practice) (8–10 minutes)

- The facilitator reviews the "why" behind this step.
- Group members discuss the implications for the leader presenter's learning or where they think the leader presenter should go next in his or her thinking based on what they've heard and discussed.
- Possible prompts:
  - "I think [leader presenter] really might want to think about . . ."
  - "I think a possible next step in [leader presenter's] learning might be . . ."
  - "Is there other evidence that can be gathered around . . . ?"
  - "What do you think about [leader presenter] trying to learn . . . ?"
- Leader presenter doesn't speak and works on active listening.

6. Consolidate Thinking and Plan Next Steps (5 minutes)

- The facilitator reviews the "why" behind this step.
- Leader presenter refers to his or her notes and summarizes what he or she is thinking (with input from the group). What resonates?
- If possible, leader presenter talks about the next best learning move.

7. Reflections on the Process (5–8 minutes)

- The facilitator reviews the "why" behind this step.
- Leader presenter reflects on his or her learning from the collaborative analysis by being asked: How did we push your thinking and add value because we were together?
- Each member of the group shares one thing that was put in his or her "parking lot" of personal connections.
- The whole group reflects on the process of using the protocol (what did/didn't work well in terms of the intended "learning conversation" objective).

References

Alig-Mielcarek, J. M. (2003). *A model of school success: Instructional leadership, academic press, and student achievement* (Doctoral dissertation, Ohio State University). Retrieved from https://etd.ohiolink.edu/!etd.send_file?accession=osu1054144000&disposition=inline

Barber, M. (2001). *From good to great: Large-scale reform in England.* Paper presented at the Futures of Education conference, Zurich.

Baskerville, D., & Goldblatt, H. (2009). Learning to be a critical friend: From professional indifference through challenge to unguarded conversations. *Cambridge Journal of Education, 39,* 205–221.

Bereiter, C., & Scardamalia, M. (1987). *The psychology of written composition.* Hillsdale, NJ: Lawrence Erlbaum.

Blackwell, L. S., Trzesniewski, K. H., & Dweck, C. S. (2007). Implicit theories of intelligence predict achievement across an adolescent transition: A longitudinal study and an intervention. *Child Development, 78,* 246–263.

Blase, J., & Blase, J. (1998). *Handbook of instructional leadership: How really good principals promote teaching and learning.* Thousand Oaks, CA: Corwin.

Bryk, A. (2015). Accelerating how we learn to improve. *Educational Researcher, 44,* 467–477.

Catmull, E. (2014, March 12). Inside the Pixar braintrust. *Fast Company.* Retrieved from http://www.fastcompany.com/3027135/lessons-learned/inside-the-pixar-braintrust

Cialdini, R. B. (2007). *Influence: The psychology of persuasion.* New York: HarperCollins.

Costa, A., & Kallick, B. (1995). Through the lens of a critical friend. In A. Costa & B. Kallick (Eds.), *Assessment in the learning organization: Shifting the paradigm* (pp. 153–156). Alexandria, VA: ASCD.

Cowan, J. (2015). The smart CEO's most undervalued skill. *Canadian Business, 88,* 4.

Darling-Hammond, L. (2000). Teacher quality and student achievement: A review of state policy evidence. *Educational Policy Analysis Archives, 8*(1). Retrieved from http://epaa.asu.edu/ojs/article/view/392/515

Donohoo, J. (2013). *Collaborative inquiry for educators.* Thousand Oaks, CA: Corwin.

Donohoo, J., & Velasco, M. (2016). *The transformative power of collaborative inquiry: Realizing change in schools and classrooms.* Thousand Oaks, CA: Corwin.

Duhigg, C. (2012). *The power of habit: Why we do what we do in life and business.* Toronto: Doubleday Canada.

Earl, L., & Katz, S. (2006a). How networked learning communities work. *Centre for Strategic Education Seminar Series Paper, 155,* 1–20.

Earl, L., & Katz, S. (2006b). *Leading schools in a data-rich world.* Thousand Oaks, CA: Corwin.

Easton, L. B. (2009). *Protocols for professional learning.* Alexandria, VA: ASCD.

Elmore, R. F. (2004). *School reform from the inside out: Policy, practice, and performance.* Cambridge, MA: Harvard University Press.

Elmore, R. F. (2007). Professional networks and school improvement. *School Administrator, 64,* 20–24.

Elmore, R. F. (Ed.). (2011). *I used to think . . . and now I think . . .* Cambridge, MA: Harvard University Press.

Ericsson, A., & Pool, R. (2016). *Peak: How to master almost anything.* Toronto: Penguin Canada.

Ericsson, K. A., Krampe, R. T., & Tesch-Römer, C. (1993). The role of deliberate practice in the acquisition of expert performance. *Psychological Review, 100,* 363–406.

Fullan, M., & Quinn, J. (2015). *Coherence: The right drivers in action for schools, systems, and districts.* Thousand Oaks, CA: Corwin.

General Teaching Council of England. (2004). *The learning conversation: Talking together for professional development.* Retrieved from http://www.gtce.org.uk/learningconversations

Gladwell, M. (2008). *Outliers: The story of success.* New York: Little, Brown.

Glaser, R., & Chi, M. (1988). Introduction: What is it to be an expert? In M. Chi, R. Glaser, & M. Farr (Eds.), *The nature of expertise* (pp. xv–xxviii). Hillsdale, NJ: Lawrence Erlbaum.

Good, C., Aronson, J., & Inzlicht, M. (2003). Improving adolescents' standardized test performance: An intervention to reduce the effects of stereotype threat. *Applied Developmental Psychology, 24,* 645–662.

Hakkarainen, K., Palonen, T., Paavola, S., & Lehtinen, E. (2004). *Communities of networked expertise: Professional and educational perspectives.* Amsterdam: Elsevier.

Hallinger, P. (2005). Instructional leadership and the school principal: A passing fancy that refuses to fade away. *Leadership and Policy in Schools, 4*(3), 221–239.

Hattie, J. (2009). *Visible learning: A synthesis of over 800 meta-analyses relating to achievement.* New York: Routledge.

Hattie, J. (2015). High impact leadership. *Educational Leadership, 72*(5), 36–40.

Hattie, J., & Timperley, H. (2007). The power of feedback. *Review of Educational Research, 77,* 81–112.

Heifetz, R., Grashow, A., & Linsky, M. (2009). *The practice of adaptive leadership: Tools and tactics for changing your organization and the world.* Boston: Cambridge Leadership Associates.

Hitt, D. H., & Tucker, P. D. (2016). Systematic review of key leadership practices found to influence student achievement: A unified framework. *Review of Educational Research, 86*(2), 531–569.

Janis, I. L. (1972). *Victims of groupthink: A psychological study of foreign-policy decisions and fiascoes.* Boston: Houghton Mifflin.

Katz, S. (2000). Competency, epistemology and pedagogy: Curriculum's holy trinity. *Curriculum Journal, 11*(2), 133–144.

Katz, S. (2002). Reconnecting the child and the curriculum: Places of paradox. *Curriculum and Teaching, 17*(1), 5–20.

Katz, S. (2010). Together is better . . . sometimes: Building and sustaining impactful learning communities within and across schools. *SDCO Connection, 1*(3), 12–13.

Katz, S., & Dack, L. A. (2009). *A learning network implementation study: The case of the GAPPRS networked learning community.* Research report for the District School Board of Niagara, St. Catherine's, ON.

Katz, S., & Dack, L. A. (2013). *Intentional interruption: Breaking down learning barriers to transform professional practice.* Thousand Oaks, CA: Corwin.

Katz, S., Earl, L., & Ben Jaafar, S. (2009). *Building and connecting learning communities: The power of networks for school improvement.* Thousand Oaks, CA: Corwin.

Kohn, N. W., & Smith, S. M. (2011). Collaborative fixation: Effects of others' ideas on brainstorming. *Applied Cognitive Psychology, 25,* 359–371.

Larson-Knight, B. (2000). Leadership, culture, and organizational learning. In K. Leithwood (Ed.), *Understanding schools as intelligent systems* (pp. 125–140). Stamford, CT: JAI Press.

Leithwood, K. (2012). *The Ontario Leadership Framework 2012 with a discussion of the research foundations.* Toronto: Institute for Education Leadership.

Leithwood, K. (2013). *Strong districts and their leadership.* Toronto: Institute for Education Leadership.

Leithwood, K., & Azah, V. N. (2014). Executive summary. In *Elementary and secondary principals' and vice-principals' workload: Final research report.* Toronto: Ontario Ministry of Education.

Leithwood, K., Day, C., Sammons, P., Harris, A., & Hopkins, D. (2006). *Successful school leadership: What it is and how it influences pupil learning.* London: Great Britain, Department for Education and Skills.

Leithwood, K., Harris, A., & Hopkins, D. (2008). Seven strong claims about successful school leadership. *School Leadership & Management, 28*(1), 27–42.

Leithwood, K., Louis, K. S., Anderson, S., & Wahlstrom, K. (2004). *How leadership influences student learning.* New York: Wallace Foundation.

Little, J. W. (1990). The persistence of privacy: Autonomy and initiative in teachers' professional relations. *Teachers College Record, 91,* 509–536.

Locke, E. A., & Lathan, G. P. (2002). Building a practically useful theory of goal setting and task motivation: A 35-year odyssey. *American Psychologist, 57,* 705–717.

Lunenburg, F. C. (2010). Group decision making: The potential for groupthink. *International Journal of Management, Business, and Administration, 13*(1), 1–6.

MacBeath, J. (1998). "I didn't know he was ill": The role and value of the critical friend. In L. Stoll & K. Myers (Eds.), *No quick fixes: Perspectives on schools in difficulty* (pp. 118–132). London: Falmer Press.

Martin, R. (2007). *The opposable mind: Winning through integrative thinking.* Cambridge, MA: Harvard Business Press.

Marzano, R., Pickering, D., & Pollock, J. (2001). *Classroom instruction that works: Research-based strategies for increasing student achievement.* Alexandria, VA: ASCD.

Matthews, G. (2015, May). *Evidence writing goals down works.* Paper presented at the Ninth Annual International Conference of the Psychology Research Unit of the Athens Institute for Education and Research Athens, Greece.

McChesney, C., Covey, S., & Huling, J. (2012). *The 4 disciplines of execution.* New York: Free Press.

McDonald, J., Mohr, N., Dichter, A., & McDonald, E. (2007). *The power of protocols: An educator's guide to better practice.* New York: Teachers College Press.

McGonigal, K. (2011). *The willpower instinct.* New York: Avery.

Mourshed, M., Chijioke, C., & Barber, M. (2010). *How the world's most improved school systems keep getting better.* N.p.: McKinsey & Company.

Nokes, T. J., Schunn, C. D., & Chi, M. T. H. (2010). Problem solving and human expertise. In P. Peterson, E. Baker, & B. McGaw (Eds.), *International encyclopedia of education* (3rd ed., Vol. 5, pp. 265–272). Oxford: Elsevier.

Nye, B., Konstantopoulos, S., & Hedges, L. V. (2004). How large are teacher effects? *Educational Evaluation and Policy Analysis, 26*(3), 237–257.

Ontario Ministry of Education. (2011). *Professional learning cycle* [DVD], *Facilitator's guide* [SS/L-18ITEB]. Toronto: Student Achievement Division, Ontario Ministry of Education.

Ontario Ministry of Education. (2012). *The Ontario Leadership Framework: A school and system leader's guide to putting Ontario's leadership framework into action.* Toronto: Institute for Education Leadership.

Pentland, A. (2015). *Social physics.* New York: Penguin.

Piaget, J. (1952). *The origins of intelligence in children* (M. Cook, Trans.). New York: International Universities Press.

Robinson, V., Hohepa, M., & Lloyd, C. (2009). *School leadership and student outcomes: Identifying what works and why—A best evidence synthesis.* Wellington: New Zealand Ministry of Education.

Robinson, V., Lloyd, C., & Rowe, K. (2008). The impact of leadership on student outcomes: An analysis of the differential effects of leadership types. *Educational Administration Quarterly, 44*(5), 635–674.

Roth, B. (2015). *The achievement habit.* New York: HarperCollins.

Snow, C. (2015). Rigor and realism: Doing educational science in the real world. *Educational Researcher, 44,* 460–466.

Supovitz, J. (2006). *The case for district-based reform: Leading, building, and sustaining school improvement.* Cambridge, MA: Harvard University Press.

Timperley, H. S. (2011). *Realizing the power of professional learning.* London: Open University Press.

Timperley, H. S., Wilson, A., Barrar, H., & Fung, I. (2008). *Teacher professional learning and development: Best evidence synthesis iteration (BES).* Wellington: New Zealand Ministry of Education.

Woolfolk, A. E., Winne, P. H., & Perry, N. E. (2015). *Educational psychology* (6th Canadian ed.). Toronto: Pearson.

Index

Accountability, 11, 52–54,
54–55 (box), 56
in leadership inquiry process,
118, 128, 150
Achievement, student, 37 (box)
and community, 47
and instructional leadership,
63, 64
and teacher practice, 42, 52 (box)
Achievement Habit, The (Roth), 18
Activity traps, 132
Aid and assistance, 74
Alig-Mielcarek, J. M., 64
"And," 18–20
Anderson, S., 41
Aronson, J., 89
Attention, 69–70
Azah, V. N., 6, 13

Balanced Literary Diet, 26
Barber, M., 20, 24, 29
Barrar, H., 4 (figure)
Baskerville, D., 19, 129
Ben Jaafar, S., 4
Bereiter, C., 123
Blackwell, L. S., 89
Blase, J., 64
Brainstorming, 76
Bryk, T., 25, 26
"But," 18

Candor, 80
Capacity building, 44, 45 (box)
Care, culture of, 8 (box), 10 (box)
Catmull, E., 80

Challenges, adaptive, 90, 93
Challenges of practice, 10–11,
12–13 (box), 87–91, 100
determining, 91–106
responding to, 104–106.
See also Leadership learning
inquiries
Change
and relationships, 44
resistance to, 77–78
and school environment, 47
Chi, M., 67, 107
Chijioke, C., 20
Cialdini, R. B., 77, 79, 82
Collaboration, 44, 73–82
default practices of, 74–79
lack of quality control in, 79
taxonomy for examining, 74
See also Leader Learning Team
(LLT) structure and process
Collaborative inquiry, 27, 37 (box),
49. *See also* Leader Learning
Team (LLT) structure
and process
*Collaborative Inquiry for
Educators* (Donohoo), 27
Collaborative leader learning.
See Leader Learning Team
(LLT) structure and process
Comfort zone, 71–73, 133
Commitments, 41–42, 49–50
Community, and student
achievement, 47
Confirmation bias, 78, 82, 142
Context, 26, 28, 56

Costa, A., 19, 129
Covey, S., 61
Cowan, J., 142
Culture of care, 8 (box),
    10 (box)
Culture of learning, 10 (box), 129
Culture of niceness, 78, 82, 131

Dack, L. A., 1, 6 (figure), 14, 19,
    27, 29, 38, 41, 43 (box),
    45 (box), 46, 47, 72, 75,
    76, 78, 88, 95, 104, 114, 115
Darley, J., 77
Darling-Hammond, L., 64
Day, C., 40
Deficit perspective, 8 (box), 51 (box)
Demand, 29, 30
Department of Education, U.S., 21
Design thinking, 18
Dichter, A., 81
Diffusion of responsibility, 76, 82
Direction, setting, 41–42,
    42–43 (box)
Discomfort, 71–73, 133
Discussions, great, 75, 77, 78–79,
    81, 82, 130
Documentation, importance of, 123
Donohoo, J., 27, 49
Duhigg, C., 69
Dweck, C. S., 89

Earl, L., 4, 15 (figure), 49, 61, 114
Easton, L. B., 81
Elmore, R., 5, 53, 78
Engagement, 27
Ericsson, A., 64
Ericsson, K. A., 61, 62, 63, 65, 66,
    67, 68, 69, 70, 71, 72
Expectations
    from above, 9–10 (box).
        See also Middle space
    establishing, 41
    intelligent, 21, 28, 32
    for students, 8 (box)
    for teaching practice, 9 (box)
Expertise, 64, 67, 72, 73, 142

Facilitator, 131
Failure, learning from, 114–115

Feedback, 70–71, 82, 142. See also
    Friendship, critical
Fixed mindset, 89
Focus, 69–70
Friendship, critical, 19, 20,
    128–129
    learning conversations protocol,
        130–152, 154–155 (figure)
    See also Collaboration; Leader
        Learning Team (LLT)
        structure and process
Fullan, M., 11
Fung, I., 4 (figure)

General Teaching Council of
    England, 81
Genovese, C., 76–77
Getting better. See Improvement
Gladwell, M., 64–65
Glaser, R., 107
Goals, 68–69
    establishing, 41
    and feedback, 70–71
    and language, 18
    monitoring, 71
Goldblatt, H., 19, 129
Good, C., 89
Grashow, A., 88
Groupthink, 75–76, 82, 141
Growth mindset, 89

Hakkarainen, K., 104
Hallinger, P., 41, 44, 46, 49
Harris, A., 40
Hattie, J., 2, 11, 22, 25, 50,
    60–61, 64, 70, 88
Hedges, L. V., 64
Heifetz, R., 88
Hitt, D. H., 41
Hohepa, M., 5
Hopkins, D., 40
How the World's Most Improved
    School Systems Keep Getting
    Better (Mourshed, Chijioke, &
    Barber), 20
Huling, J., 61

Ideas, opposing, 18
Impact, evaluating, 60–61

Improvement
  desire for, 61
  DNA of, 66–67
  monitoring, 96
  and purposeful practice, 62–66
  working for, 61–62
  See also School improvement
Inclusion, 31
Indicators, 61
Influence, 39, 40, 50, 55, 56, 59, 91,
  97, 100
Initiatives, 13
Inquiries, leadership learning.
  See Leadership learning
  inquiries
Inquiry, collaborative, 27, 37 (box),
  49. *See also* Leader Learning
  Team (LLT) structure and
  process
Inquiry habit of mind, 61
Institute of Education Sciences, 21
Instruction
  focused approach to, 22
  improving, 48–50, 50–52 (box)
  See also Practice, teacher
Instructional guidance system, 23
Integrative thinking, 23
Intentional Interruption (Katz &
  Dack), 1–2, 3, 5, 14, 19, 29, 78,
  95, 104
Interruptions, intentional, 18, 136,
  142, 146. See also *Intentional
  Interruption*
Inzlicht, M., 89
I Used To Think…and Now I Think
  (Elmore), 5

Janis, I., 75
Joint work, 74–79
Judgment, professional, 13, 21, 28, 29

Kallick, B., 19, 129
Katz, S., 1, 4, 6 (figure), 11, 13, 14, 15,
  15 (figure), 19, 27, 29, 38, 41, 43
  (box), 45 (box), 46, 47, 49, 61,
  72, 74, 75, 76, 77, 78, 79, 88, 95,
  104, 114, 115, 123, 130, 132
Knowledge, production vs.
  application, 25–26

Knowledge mobilization, 29, 30
Knowledge transformation, 123
Kohn, N. W., 76
Konstantopoulos, S., 64
Krampe, R. T., 64

Language, and approach
  to goals, 18
Larson-Knight, B., 64
Latané, Bibb, 77
Lathan, G. P., 68
Leader, inquiry-minded, 61
Leader Learning Team (LLT)
  structure and process, 59, 60
  accountability in, 118, 128, 150
  culture of learning in, 129
  described, 86–87
  implementation of, 86
  learning conversations protocol,
    130–152, 154–155 (figure)
  mechanics of, 127–128
  meeting facilitators, 131
  meeting norms, 133–134
  meetings, 130–152
  meeting schedule, 127–128
  psychological foundations of,
    73–74
  variability within, 97
  See also Leadership learning
    inquiry template
Leaders, teacher, 45 (box), 54 (box)
Leadership, instructional, 2, 63, 64
Leadership, intelligent, 40
Leadership, literal, 14
Leadership, responsive, 40
Leadership, school. *See* School
  leadership
Leadership inquiry questions,
  91–106
Leadership learning inquiries,
  87–91
  completing, 124
  focus of, 95
  framework for, 104 (box)
  framework for, revised, 105–106,
    105–106 (box)
  "how" of, 103–106
  intent of, 115
  learning cases, 101–102

transferability of learning in,
102–103
"what" of, 94–100
"who" of, 100–103
See also Leader Learning
Team (LLT) structure and
process; Leadership inquiry
questions; Leadership
learning inquiry template;
Learning moves
Leadership learning inquiry
template, 91–106, 117 (box),
125 (figure)
embedding professional learning
cycle into, 106–107, 108–110
(figure), 111–114
need for, 118, 123
planning in, 107
Leadership practices
building relationships, 44–46
and context, 56
enacting, 56
improving instructional
program, 48–50, 50–52 (box)
organization development, 46–48
securing accountability, 53–54,
54–55 (box)
setting direction, 41–42,
42–43 (box)
Leading indicators, 61
Learning
vs. doing, 106, 124, 146
from failure, 114–115
and relationships, 44
Learning, culture of, 10 (box), 129
Learning, new, 1–2
Learning, permanent, 102
Learning, professional, 1–2
collaborative inquiry, 27,
37 (box), 49. *See also* Leader
Learning Team (LLT)
structure and process;
Leadership learning
inquiries
cycle of, 4 (figure), 106–107,
108–110 (figure), 111–114
determining kind needed,
36 (box)

leadership and, 5–6, 38
and permanence, 5
school improvement and, 3–5
supportive conditions for,
36 (box)
teacher practice and, 3–5, 38, 49
as well-being strategy, 45
Learning, real, 1–2, 3
Learning cases, 101–102
Learning conversations, 81–82
Learning conversations protocol,
130–152, 154–155 (figure)
Learning culture, 42 (box), 45 (box)
Learning disabilities, 31
Learning inquiries. *See* Leadership
learning inquiries
Learning moves, 102, 106
assessing intended learning
from, 112–113
defining, 111
describing, 112
monitoring, 115–116
planning, 107, 111–113
reflecting on, 113–114
small/narrow, 115–116, 118,
119–122 (box)
Lehtinen, E., 104
Leithwood, K., 6, 13, 22–23, 40, 41,
42, 44, 47, 48, 56
Linsky, M., 88
Listening, active, 142
Little, J. W., 74
Lloyd, C., 5, 44
LLT (Leader Learning Team)
structure and process. *See*
Leader Learning Team (LLT)
structure and process
Locke, E. A., 68
Louis, K. S., 41
Lunenburg, F. C., 76

MacBeath, J., 19, 129
Martin, R., 18
Marzano, R., 64
Matthews, G., 123
McChesney, C., 61, 153
McDonald, E., 81
McDonald, J., 81

McGonigal, K., 71
McKinsey Consulting, 20
Middle space
    challenges experienced in, 6–7,
        7–10 (box), 10–11,
        11–12 (box). *See also*
        Challenges of practice
    described, 2
Mindset, fixed vs. growth, 89
Mission, 41
Mohr, N., 81
Monitoring, 71, 96, 115–116
Motivation, 27
Mourshed, M., 20

Niceness, culture of, 78, 82, 131
Nokes, T. J., 67
Nye, B., 64

Ontario Leadership Framework
    (OLF), 39–41, 53
Ontario Ministry of Education, 39,
    41, 44, 46, 47, 48, 49, 105
Opposable Mind, The (Martin), 18
Organization, development of,
    46–48
Outcomes. *See* Achievement,
    student
Outliers (Gladwell), 64–65

Paavola, S., 104
Palonen, T., 104
Parents, and student
    achievement, 47
Pentland, A., 81
Permanence, 5
Perry, N. E., 27
Piaget, J., 66
Pickering, D., 64
Pixar, 80
Planning process, importance of, 107
PLC (professional learning
    community), 89–90
Pollock, J., 64
Pool, R., 61, 62, 63, 65, 66, 67, 68, 69,
    70, 71, 72
Practice, classroom. *See* Practice,
    teacher

Practice, naive, 63, 65, 67
Practice, purposeful, 62–66,
    104, 123
    and discomfort, 71–73
    and feedback, 70–71
    and focus, 69–70
    and goals, 68–69
Practice, teacher
    expectations for, 9 (box)
    impact of, 64
    improving, 48–50, 50–52 (box)
    intelligent/expected, 24–25
    and professional learning, 3–5, 38
    and student achievement,
        42, 52 (box)
Practice sessions, length of, 70
Prescription, 13, 20–21, 23, 24, 28
Pressures, 11–12 (box). *See also*
    Middle space
Principals. *See* Leadership
    practices; School leadership
Pro/con lists, 19
Professional judgment, 13, 21, 28, 29
Professional learning community
    (PLC), 89–90
Professional learning cycle,
    4 (figure), 106–107,
    108–110 (figure), 111–114
Progress, monitoring, 71
Pro/pro lists, 19
Protocols, 81–82
    learning conversations protocol,
        130–152, 154–155 (figure)

Quinn, J., 11

Relationships, 44–46, 45 (box)
Resources, 49–50, 51 (box)
Responsibility, 53
    diffusion of, 76, 82
    See also Accountability
Responsive conditions, 30, 40
    creating, 39
    and enacting leadership
        practices, 56
    See also School, intelligent
        responsive; School,
        responsive

Robinson, V., 5, 7, 11, 41, 44, 49, 50, 63
Roth, B., 18
Rowe, K., 44

Sammons, P., 40
Scardamalia, M., 123
Schemas, 66, 73
School, intelligent, 22, 28–31, 32 (table)
School, intelligent responsive, 3, 28–31, 32 (table)
School, responsive, 26–31, 32 (table)
School culture, 38, 45 (box)
School improvement
  as intentional interruption, 2
  path of, 6 (figure)
  professional learning and, 3–5
  See also Improvement
School leadership
  challenges to, 6–15
  characteristics of, 39–40. See also Leadership practices
  enabling of professional learning, 5–6, 38
  evaluating impact of, 60–61
  growth from emergent to proficient, 15, 15 (box)
  implementation challenges, 10–11, 12–13 (box). See also Challenges of practice
  initiativitis and, 13
  and instructional leadership, 2
  intelligent/responsive, 32
  literal leadership, 14
  Ontario Leadership Framework, 39–41, 53
  See also Influence
Schunn, C. D., 67
Setting direction, 41–42, 42–43 (box)
Sharing, 74
Smith, S. M., 76

Snow, C., 21, 25
Social loafing, 77
Staff, 45–46, 49
Storytelling and scanning for ideas, 74
Strategies, high-yield, 25
Superfice, culture of, 131
Supovitz, J., 73, 79
Supply, 29
Supports, 13
System Implementation and Monitoring (SIM), 71

Teacher practice. See Practice, teacher
Teachers, 45–46, 49
Teaching. See Practice, teacher
10,000-hour rule, 64–65
Tesch-Römer, C., 64
Timperley, H. S., 4 (figure), 70, 87
Trailing indicators, 61
Transferability, of learning, 102–103
Trzesniewski, K. H., 89
Tucker, P. D., 41

Understanding, deep, 67, 73, 95, 130–131, 142
Urgency, sense of, 45 (box)

Velasco, M., 49
Visible Learning (Hattie), 22
Vision, establishing, 41

Wahlstrom, K., 41
What Works Clearinghouse (WWC), 21–22, 25
Willows, D., 26
Wilson, A., 4 (figure)
Winne, P. H., 27
Wins, small, 69, 116
Woolfolk, A. E., 27, 68, 69, 71, 123
Work, joint, 74–79
Writing process, influence of, 123

A SAGE Publishing Company

Helping educators make the greatest impact

CORWIN HAS ONE MISSION: to enhance education through intentional professional learning.

We build long-term relationships with our authors, educators, clients, and associations who partner with us to develop and continuously improve the best evidence-based practices that establish and support lifelong learning.

ONTARIO PRINCIPALS' COUNCIL
Exemplary Leadership in Public Education

The Ontario Principals' Council (OPC) is a voluntary association for principals and vice-principals in Ontario's public school system. We believe that exemplary leadership results in outstanding schools and improved student achievement. To this end, we foster quality leadership through world-class professional services and supports. As an ISO 9001 registered organization, we are committed to **"quality leadership—our principal product."**

Made in the USA
Monee, IL
20 September 2021